BEST FACE FORWARD

MARILYN MIGLIN

D1053973

CHICAGO SPECTRUM PRESS
LOUISVILLE, KENTUCKY 40207

© 2002 by Marilyn Miglin

CHICAGO SPECTRUM PRESS
4824 BROWNSBORO CENTER
LOUISVILLE, KENTUCKY 40207
502-899-1919

All rights reserved. Except for appropriate use in critical reviews or works of scholarship, the reproduction or use of this work in any form or by any electronic, mechanical, or other means now known or here-after invented, including photocopying and recording, and in any information storage and retrieval system, is forbidden without written permission of the author.

Printed in the U.S.A.

10 9 8 7 6 5 4 3 2 1

ISBN:1-886094-68-3

To order more copies of this book, contact:
The Marilyn Miglin Institute
1-800-662-1120
or visit www.marilynmiglin.com

Cover: Skrebneski photograph

This book is dedicated to Lee Miglin, whom I shall miss for the rest of my life. I will always love and remember you.

ACKNOWLEDGMENTS

There are so many people who have played an important role in helping me to become the person I am today. Without them, my adventures and this book would not be possible. . .

To my "three graces," Helen, Virge, and Marion. To my children, Marlena and Duke, who have given their parents much to be proud of. To my sweet sister-in-law, Gladys, who dedicated ten years of her life in caring for my mother-in-law. To Carl Miglin, a very devoted brother-in-law. To my favorite Uncle George. To my wonderful nephew Mike Wilfong, whose dedication to my mother and aunt will never be forgotten. To my sweet Jadwiga Malek, a special member of the Miglin family for over twenty-nine years. To the Hartman family with love. To Dorsey and John, both of whom I miss very much. To Eugene Martello, for always being there. To my good friend and perfumer, Vito Lenoci, who has believed in me and helped my olfactory esteem. To my lovely Joanne Benjamin, a perfect Home Shopping "banana." To Arlene Jurinek for my special times in the sky. To Dan Davis for his dedication, perseverance, and passionate belief in my dreams. To my loyal staff, who have been through so many changes in my ever growing and evolving company. To Judy Niedermaier for her years of friendship and support. To Marshall Bennett, who helped me through a time of unbelievable darkness. To Abel Berland, I shall never forget our lunches together. To Ralph Fujimoto and Lyric Hughes, the future is ours. To "Kup," my Uncle Irv. To Alderman Natarus, who helps make Chicago work. To John Renfrow and my wonderful Special Services friends, who keep my frenetic travel schedule in good order. To Charles Ettner, who keeps me cool. To Al and Susie Friedman for being such nice partners. To Al Kraml, for keeping everything perfect. To Bill Gahlberg, a long-time family friend. To Victor Skrebneski for his friendship and photography. To Carol Watkins, a girl for all "seasons." To Ken Beachler, my special dancing partner. To Bill Zwecker, a lifelong friend. To Nena Ivon, my Libra twin and Hazel "Legs" Barr. To Pam Lassers, a true friend. To Camylle DeLaurentis for keeping the humor. To Ann Gerber, for always nice words. To Marlene Rubenstein for her energy, energy, energy. To Mary Jo Filippini, a fine friend who keeps me smiling. To Helen Umbdenstock for her positive energy. To Ming, who makes me look better in clothes. To Lesley Spencer, my music connection. To Heather Webster, a formidable vice president of wealth. To Barry Axler, my favorite rabbi. To Dennis Carlin, a wonderful "Lee Miglin" choice. To Mr. Vivian for driving "Miss Daisy." To Dorothy Kavka, for answering every one of Lee's questions. To Janet Lindsey, who makes Mauna Kea Magic. To every single one of my special, loyal customers— you are my extended family. And to everyone I have met along life's highway who has given to me something of themselves, thank you and until we meet again. . . .

This book is about the "magic of believing." Throughout my life, I have been blessed with a special gift for positive thinking, an inability to say "no," an innate need to accept nothing less than the best, and an appetite for adventure.

If you believe in yourself and in your dreams, if you look for the magic and embrace the positive energy all around, then you will understand this book.

CHAPTER ONE

"Success is to laugh often and much, to win the respect of intelligent people and the appreciation of honest critics, to endure the betrayal of false friends, to appreciate beauty, to find the best in others and to leave the world a bit better—whether by a healthy child, a garden patch or a redeemed social condition—to know that even one life has breathed easier because you have lived. This is to have succeeded."

If you can't succeed in Chicago, you can't succeed anywhere. It's a city that gets into your heart and soul. It is so much a part of my life that, although I have traveled the world over, I can still think of no finer place in which to live.

This is a city that is made up of culturally diverse neighborhoods, a strong Midwest work ethic, and a special appreciation of its own beauty. It has given me life, education, love, and family. Much of my life's story takes place here, and if you have ever lived in or visited my city, you already know a lot about me.

I was born in Chicago's Pilsen neighborhood, a place of small bungalows and "walk-up" apartment buildings. I was an only child, although I had some boy cousins, aunts, and uncles.

When I was three years old, we moved to the northwest side, to a neighborhood of three-story apartment buildings and concrete. Not many people knew one another, as the area was comprised of mostly transient families.

My father, Frank "Skip" Klecka, was the third of five sons born into a Czech family of six children. A kind and gentle man, he was a romantic at heart. I believe he won my mother's heart with the passionate poetry he wrote to her.

Years later, as I read these poems, I could see how easy it would be for my mother to fall in love with him. He was a handsome, free-spirited, athletic man with a light complexion and dark blonde hair.

My mother, Helen, was the youngest of three sisters and one brother. Her mother, my grandmother, was a woman with courage and far ahead of her time when she packed up her children and left an abusive husband who had a drinking problem.

Both she and my mother had the same kind of personality—opinionated. They *loved* to argue. When you grow up with two such strong women you either talk back or learn to surrender. I like to believe that I received my inner strength from the two of them.

Helen was a latchkey child and her upbringing was not exceptionally happy. But she was bright and her enthusiasm for life was contagious.

She saw herself as a "glamour" girl and found her escape from problems at home through the movies. It was the time of the great romantic Hollywood stars, such as Joan Crawford, Claudette Colbert, and Jean Harlow, and Helen tried to emulate their style. She was the life of any party, a good dancer, and pretty enough that she turned heads wherever she went.

Skip and Helen were a carefree, adventurous couple with an incredible zest for life—swimming in abandoned quarries, exploring the city by motorcycle, my mother holding on to the back of my father, and partying with friends.

My mother and grandmother always had a strong influence on my life, and Helen was determined that I would succeed on a level her own generation had never known.

She insisted that I learn to read at an early age by encouraging me to recite fairy tales aloud. While Helen washed dishes or engaged in other housework, I would read to her the story of *Snow White* or my favorite books, *Cinderella, the Little Engine That Could, Scat, Scat, Go Away Little Cat* and *Bambi,* which always made me cry.

Her enthusiastic embrace of Hollywood musicals and their glamour became part of my world as well. She adored the Ziegfield showgirls and dancers and often, in lieu of lullabies, sang to me the romantic songs she learned from movies and the radio.

Helen had her own charismatic style of glamour. She understood the artful use of makeup and during World War II, she was the only housewife on our street to receive prime cuts of meat and the best produce. There never seemed to have been any rationing in our household.

Helen always looked her best; she smiled flirtatiously while wearing her pretty makeup and settled for nothing less than the best.

Through Helen's eyes, I developed an appreciation for glamour and flirtation at an unusually early age. When I was four, she enrolled me in tap-dancing lessons.

Certain that my legs were to be long and beautiful like Marlene Dietrich's, Helen set forth a regime of dance, and then drama, for added poise. Each evening, she carefully set my hair when she prepared me for bed, instilling in me the grooming rituals that I still follow today.

My parents with me, age four

I was a little girl born to please—taught never to swear, and never to question my parents' requests. Cultivating the manners with which I had been so carefully raised, I learned to say "please" and "thank you," and always to smile. I was an obedient child, who understood the difference between right and wrong and always chose the right way of doing things.

I remember my father taking me for long walks as he taught me the Bohemian tradition of mushroom picking. It was a magical experience for me when we returned home with our harvest, which we dried atop a screen so that Helen could use them in whatever she was cooking.

My father also took me fishing, and he would laugh when I said, "Daddy, please use bread for bait instead of those poor worms." When we caught catfish, to Helen's dismay, we would put them in the bathtub to keep them alive.

Sometimes my father and I would find arrowheads, and then he would tell me wonderful stories about the Native Americans who had lived around the Great Lakes. We often visited his friend's farm in Huntley, Illinois, where I would ride the tractors and horses. I even learned to milk a cow.

My father was a wonderful storyteller and he would make up detective stories to enthrall my friends and me. With his soft, melodious voice that mimicked the radio announcers of the time, his tales were so vivid and realistic that he once frightened my cousin Denny into having terrible nightmares.

I loved make-believe.

I had my dolls, who lived in an enchanted doll house and I carefully drew fashions, dressing my ladies elegantly in my own couture creations. I loved to draw and fancied myself a real artist. With my paper and crayons, I could go anywhere and do anything.

There were constantly new lessons to be learned, new friends to make, new experiences to be analyzed, and new information to digest.

"Someday I will buy you a real horse," my father promised, and my imagination would fly—Marilyn, the little princess, gracefully cantering past her playmates, sidesaddle, of course. Oh, I could hardly wait until that time. I even took riding lessons and loved them!

We lived a modestly comfortable life until, when I was eleven years old, my father died. He was only thirty-eight years old.

Not only did I lose the most important man in my life, but his death changed my life in many other ways. There is only one death and that is the first. With that trauma, certain basic emotions are wrenched from you forever. For me, nothing was ever again the same.

That year, I had been promoted a grade and being much younger than the rest of my class, I already felt alone and out of place. When I returned to school the week after his death, I was so self-conscious. I could feel the exaggerated stares of the other children, and I imagined them whispering about me. I was very different now—my comfort had been torn away from me and I felt that I was unlike any other eleven year old at that time.

My father died of tuberculosis. While that may not sound very dramatic today, when I was a child, to have such a diagnosis meant whispered telephone conversations and raised eyebrows. TB was a contagious disease for which there was no cure.

He was sick for a very long time, coughing and losing weight. "It's just a bad cold," he would say so that he could stay with us and continue to work.

My mother would tell people, "Skip has a little rheumatism."

As he began to lose his strength, his employers, not knowing the real reason for his exhaustion, agreed to allow my father to leave work earlier than usual.

When his disease became exacerbated by a case of food poisoning, he was taken by ambulance and admitted to the Municipal Tuberculosis Sanitarium located on Pulaski Road, between Peterson and Bryn Mawr Avenues on the far northwest side of the city. Situated in a beautiful park-like setting, the hospital used the most up-to-date method of treatment available in order to "cure" patients—treatments such as forcing them to breathe cold air and sometimes even collapsing the infected lung.

Today, antibiotics are used to cure TB. The Sanitarium buildings with their extensive grounds have been turned into senior citizen housing and a nature center.

Even when my father was admitted to the Sanitarium, Helen told people he was in the hospital, taking care not to mention which one. When she went to visit him, I accompanied her on the long bus ride.

Since I was not allowed into the building where he was, she sat me in a tavern across the street from the Sanitarium, asking the owner to allow me to stay there while she visited my father.

"I'll be back soon to get you," she would say.

It was a different era, and I never felt threatened by being in a tavern with strangers. The fellows talked to me and would buy me Cokes. I think that is where I learned how to talk to men naturally, even though I was still a very shy ten-and-one-half year old girl.

Because of the highly contagious nature of TB, my father's coroner's report set off alarm bells with the local departments of health and child welfare. Although Helen sterilized everything in our apartment, boiling the silverware and scouring surfaces, the Department of Health had no idea that we had lived with my father's illness for so long. They were very concerned with my safety.

In one of the most terrifying moments of my childhood, a social worker actually attempted to separate Helen and me, reasoning that it was not safe for me to live at home. After all, my mother could have contracted the disease, thereby putting me in immediate danger as well.

"No one will ever take me away," I protested. "If you take me away from here, I will run away and come back." This was not a threat, but a real promise.

Helen described in detail to the social worker the precautions she had taken while my father was at home—and there was no way that the state worker could have pried me from home or my family's arms. It became quickly apparent that there was absolutely no way of winning this contest and she left. Needless to say, Helen and I were very relieved.

Somehow life went on. It had to. There was simply no other alternative.

There are, I have learned, no victories without conflicts, and no rainbows without storms. With my father gone, everything was different. We still would get up every morning as we had always done, and I would go to school each day, but it was not the same as before.

Unfortunately, without the luxury of insurance, there were bills to pay and we had to eat. So, two weeks after my father died, Helen walked four blocks from our home to the O'Bryan Brother's Lingerie Company, applied for a job, and was hired as a key punch operator.

I became a latchkey child.

Each day, after school, I cleaned the house and started dinner. In between, I managed to squeeze in my homework. Helen did her best to support us, but there was still almost no money.

I was only eleven, but I lied about my age and got my first job as a nurse's aide at Belmont Hospital. Helen was not happy about my starting work so young, but we needed the extra bit of money I earned.

It was there that I learned the meaning of compassion—or in many instances the lack of it. I always believed that kindness and empathy were so important, especially to a sick person.

It was now my mother, her two sisters, and my grandmother who became the center of my life. My Aunt Virge was the "intellectual," Marion was the "society aunt," and Helen, was the "glamour girl." These were my Three Graces, the three wise women who guided me. My grandmother, the matriarch, continued to reinforce all of the "proper" ladylike qualities in me, in addition to teaching me more down-to-earth lessons such as how to bake bread, sew, iron, and wash floors. A part of each of them became a part of who I am.

After my father died, there were no more men to whom I could look. I had my wonderful Uncle Jimmy, the husband of my Aunt Virge, who always made me laugh, but he died soon

Twelve years old, at a family party

after my father. So, I began my new life in a world of women as a young eighth grader—very tall, very thin, and very self-conscious.

Rarely did I venture from my own neighborhood, but shortly after my father's death, my friend Karen Oppenheim and her parents asked my mother if they could take me to visit Karen's aunt who lived in Glencoe, a wealthy North Shore suburb of Chicago.

I remember Karen and me in the car, giggling and laughing as girls do. But when we reached Glencoe and I stepped from the car, I decided that this life-style would be my goal.

The house was the most beautiful I had ever seen. Ivy scaled the walls and a private, curving driveway welcomed us. Colorful and fragrant flowers dotted the landscape around not only the front of the house, but the driveway and surrounding wooded area as well.

We knocked on the door, and a maid answered. Of course, I had never seen a maid's uniform before. As we were escorted inside, Karen's aunt greeted us. With my very best manners, I shook her hand and said, "Thank you for inviting me. You have such a beautiful house." Never was a polite phrase more passionately spoken.

When Karen went upstairs to use the bathroom, I followed her.

Suddenly, I was aware that there was another story to the house! Never before had I been inside a house with a second floor. And there were beautiful flowers in the bathroom. It was all so elegant and glamorous.

I decided at that moment, one day when I was able to do so, I would have a house that would have two stories or even more, and that my bathroom, too, would be adorned with fresh flowers.

My expectations in life changed that day.

Helen told me that there was a reason for everything. Through all the difficulties she encountered, she remained an optimist. Because of her strength and determination, I was able to see the bright side to many difficult situations. The greatest gift I received from her was a positive, mental attitude.

"There is absolutely nothing you cannot do or achieve," she told me. "You have a special light."

Helen never really pampered me or bestowed upon me much praise in public. No one other than my immediate family knew about my outstanding school grades. It was just something that was not touted so as not to be viewed as bragging—or to my superstitious family, a means to bring bad luck. Yet, I knew she was proud of what I did and that she loved me very much.

The safety of my new home life with Helen, however, did not compensate for the emotional agony I felt at school. Rather than blossoming into an ordinary teenager, I kept growing taller.

I was very thin, and self-conscious. Worse still was my complexion. I was sure everyone was staring at me. Everything I did seemed to worsen my condition and humiliated me further. Beautiful clear-skinned department store saleswomen at the cosmetics counter offered advice, eager for an easy sale from the teenager who hid her face, and I tried everything imaginable. Still, nothing worked and I became more withdrawn in social situations, embarrassed as only a teenager can be over blemishes I imagined to be the size of mountains. My grandmother even prayed and lit candles to St. Therese, asking for a clear skin for me.

During my first day at Schurz High School, I was so nervous I forgot my program and had to walk back home, eight blocks away.

Soon thereafter, I applied for a part-time job as a cashier and sales clerk at a clothing shop, again lying about my age. I eagerly accepted the position specifically for the holiday season in order to earn additional Christmas money. After New Year's, however, the man who had originally hired me called to ask if I would like to work after school hours. The application he gave me to complete required my date of birth, and I did not know what to do.

I took the papers home and told Helen, "Something terrible has happened! I lied to this man about my age and he's going to be upset when he finds out. What shall I do?"

Very simply, she said, "You go back tomorrow, Marilyn, and tell him you lied. Apologize, and thank him for offering you this special opportunity."

All day long in school I could hardly concentrate, I was so upset. Finally, three o'clock came and the school bell rang. I walked slowly to the bus stop.

When I saw the personnel director, I said, "I must apologize to you. I lied about my age. I am only twelve and I cannot work for you anymore. I am so sorry."

I was very, very nervous.

Amazingly, at least to me, he was unconcerned and sighed, "Well, Marilyn, that's not such a problem. We like you and your work, so we'll get you a work permit."

Beyond the relief I felt, I learned an important lesson—never tell a lie. It is always easier to tell the truth. The truth keeps one free of guilt and assists us in obtaining what we seek in life.

In June of 1953, when I was a high school sophomore, Helen and I moved to a new neighborhood closer to my high school. I became friends with our landlord's daughter, Jackie, who happened to be a professional hula dancer. I loved to dance and Jackie taught me to hula, which we practiced each day.

When I danced, the world around me seemed different. I felt beautiful and free. I was no longer the tall shy girl with bad skin.

In addition to working after school and on Saturdays, I worked in school as well for my biology teacher and for my physical education instructor. Since I was close to two years younger than my classmates, I did not have any boyfriends. I did enjoy school and joined every possible committee I could. I especially loved theater and debate classes.

One day, my physical education teacher shared with our class news of an audition for a dance scholarship. As it turned out, she had a sister who was one of the premier ballet teachers in the United States—Edna McRae.

Her dance studio was in the Fine Arts Building on Michigan Avenue, just south of the Art Institute. It was a place where many hopeful young dancers, artists, and musicians began their training. My high school teacher saw within me not only a passionate desire to dance, but a sincerity, and she arranged for me to audition for a working scholarship with Miss McRae.

Edna McRae would forever change my life.

With great enthusiasm, I relentlessly practiced my hula routine over and over. On the day of the audition, I carefully packed my hula record under my arm, hopped aboard the el train and made my way downtown to Edna's dance studio at Michigan Avenue and Van Buren. I was not necessarily nervous, as I did not quite know what to expect, but I was determined.

When the time came, I proudly presented my hula record and took my place on the floor. The music started and I began fluidly dipping my arms and hands, gracefully swiveling my hips.

Edna McRae's eyes widened and when I finished, everyone on the studio floor was quiet until she broke the silence.

"Young lady, do you realize that this is a ballet school? No one has *ever* come to my studio and auditioned by doing the hula!"

"Yes," I answered, "but I don't know ballet and I would very much like to learn. I would like to become a dancer."

Edna narrowed her eyes and demurred, "You really do like to dance, don't you."

I nodded.

"Well," she concluded, "it's obvious that you have great passion. I shall accept you on one condition—that you work for me as a secretary. I understand from my sister, that your secretarial skills are very good."

And so, as a result of my hula dancing, I was accepted into a two-year intensive dance program, which would forever after affect my entire being.

Edna McRae was a middle-aged, matronly woman with pretty white hair and glasses. She had a strong laugh, waddled like a duck, and had an extraordinary presence. Despite her full-figured girth, she could tap-dance like no one else, making the most glorious sounds. With her tap shoes on, she was unstoppable.

Every day after school, I rode the el train to Miss McRae's studio, where I worked as a secretary, taking dance classes in between my office duties. I could not have been happier for the opportunity to dance and to learn. Edna was a brilliant taskmaster. She was talented, tough, and sometimes, she could be downright mean. I learned from her not only the art of dance, but other lessons in life, including discipline and tenacity.

Miss McRae constantly berated and humiliated me in front of others. She challenged me and did her best to break me. In doing so, she ignited a passion within me that made me more determined than ever to succeed. I was quite disciplined and focused in the secretarial work I did for her, but at first I did not understand what I was supposed to learn about dance.

Edna McRae always wanted more.

You were never to speak, never to cry, and never to think about *anything* other than what you were doing at that moment. My hair was to be pulled back into a smooth bun without any curls or stray wisps out of place. Any trace of emotion was cause for a stern lecture about discipline. This is how ballet was taught at the time, and she carefully trained her dancers in the traditional "old Russian" ways.

Some of my duties included keeping the vast studio clean, and ensuring that the shades were positioned properly so that the dancers would not have light in their eyes. It was also my job to dampen the floor for added traction.

In my own classes, I learned the fundamental rules of ballet, such as to point my toe in the right direction and keep my knees facing out.

One day, soon after I started, I took my place at the barre and waited to begin. While I stood there wondering why Miss McRae was hesitating, I suddenly became aware that everybody was looking at me.

She asked, "Are you missing something? What is the matter with you? Have you not been asked time and time again to fix the shades?"

"But I did fix them," I stammered.

"When?"

"About fifteen minutes ago."

"Don't you know the sun changes position?" she demanded. "Fix those shades. We will not begin this class until you have adjusted those shades for these dancers and their eyes."

I fixed the shades and felt humiliated because she had singled me out in front of the whole class. Worse yet, there were at least twenty professional dancers from New York in the room.

Finally, we began.

In the ballet warm-up, a dancer holds onto the barre, and begins in first position, then moves on to each position through fifth. At one point, everyone was standing there with her toe touching the inside of her knee and her knee turned outward toward the mirror. As the token novice, I was the only one with my knee facing *forward*.

Suddenly, the music stopped.

Miss McRae said, "Everyone look at the stork; we have a stork in the class."

At first, I had no idea she was talking about me. I was confused by her sarcasm, and then humiliated. Everybody in the room stopped warming up, looked at me, and laughed. But she didn't stop there.

"Marilyn's grandfather must have had terrible legs," she announced, "because her legs are so skinny. Look how she's standing like a stork. Open your eyes! Look at everybody's knees, and now look at your own. Can you not see this? Are you blind?"

Of course she was correct in that I wasn't looking and had never thought to. I was deep inside myself and so happy that I was *in* a dance class. Although Miss McRae's instruction was designed to teach me to look outside myself and to learn from those around me, at times it was done with little regard for my feelings.

The next two years were so grim that I wished something terrible would happen to her. Taking the el to the studio, my stomach would tighten as the train began its descent into the subway, inching its way closer to downtown. I often hoped she would be unable to come to class at all. That was how much I hated her teaching methods. Male dancers at the studio with previous military experience swore that nothing they encountered in basic training equaled any day with Edna McRae.

Yet, I continued to return each day. It was all about dance, and that was what mattered most to me.

Another one of my duties while working for Edna involved making bank deposits for the studio. Each day, I looked forward to my walk to the First National Bank on Monroe and Dearborn. Miss McRae was a member of the First National's exclusive private banking services, which afforded me entrance into what seemed at that time like another world.

Mahogany desks, rich red leather chairs, and beautiful chandeliers accented a quiet space of luxury and sophistication that made a lasting impression upon me. I was fascinated with the elegant, wealthy women I saw—their hair perfectly coiffed, their wardrobe stylish and chic. I vowed that one day, I, too, would be part of that same world.

Edna McRae also managed what was referred to as her "line," a dance unit that performed at hotels, trade shows, and other events. It was during those shows that I began to use theatrical makeup to cover my skin and in doing so, I discovered a wonderful new confidence. My complexion looked flawless.

Edna thought it wise for me to take drama classes and voice instruction, as well. "You never know when you're going to have to belt out a couple of songs in a show," she said.

To her, a dancer needed every skill that the theater demanded and she recommended that I take instruction from Everett Clark, who was also located in the Fine Arts Building, one floor above Miss McRae. So in between classes, and while also working for Edna, I now used what little spare spending money I had to take classes with Mr. Clark, who also awarded me a working scholarship.

Everett Clark was the voice of Chicago broadcasting and the original "Whistler" on the radio program of the same name. His was the one voice that mattered in radio.

An assertive man of German heritage, slightly balding with gray hair and intense blue eyes, Everett was not handsome; he was much too severe looking for television, but that voice!

He was not quite as tyrannical with his students as Edna McRae, but was every bit as forceful and dictatorial, although he did have a sense of humor that tempered his pronouncements. He was the most formidable man I have ever met in my life. With a booming God-like voice and exaggerated mannerisms, he was a mountain of a man—barrel-chested, magnificently resonant, and equally intimidating.

According to Everett, awkward hands hindered and destroyed one's magnetic energy. He also believed in "personal magnetism."

"My Gaawd!" he would admonish me, flipping his hand in the air for added drama. "You're awful! Take that jingling-jangling jewelry off this instant! You don't need accessories. They are only the props you use to hide your tiny voice! What is wrong with your voice that you do not wish for us to hear it? My Gaawd! You squeal and you squeak. Do you think you have a voice? Speak up! Speak up!"

The man frightened me to death.

Everett had a unique "mastery" over his students, which included businessmen who wished to improve their speaking abilities. He told people how to live every aspect of their lives and they listened.

From Everett Clark I developed techniques which became an integral part of who I am today. His presence in my life allowed me opportunities to perform during the summer under his direction through the American Assembly Service, a regional agency.

One such production, *Four Centuries of American Popular Song,* afforded me a chance to tour the midwest United States, although most of our work was done in Michigan, Illinois, Indiana, and Iowa. When we had no performances on weekends, I would usually return to Chicago by bus—or to Davenport, where I taught dance.

Each song in the show portrayed a different period in American history, from the Native Americans in the 15th Century through the colonial period, the Gay Nineties, and World Wars I and II. Ragtime, jazz, and swing numbers had specialized dance routines that required a lot of time to learn.

Rehearsal for summer tour—I am on the far left

I enjoyed seeing the country while traveling on tour. The small towns in which we performed treated us as celebrities, and aspiring students sought our advice as to how they too could enter show business.

Because a dancer requires constant practice, even when on tour, I found a ballet school in Davenport, Iowa, called "Madame Veda's School of Ballet." Madame Veda felt that I was too advanced in dance to be taking her classes, so she engaged me as a teacher for her ballet classes every Saturday.

Madame Veda lived in a trailer park with her ashen gray husband. In addition to running a ballet school, she also happened to be a palmist.

"Madame Veda, I would love to learn how to read palms," I said. "Will you teach me?"

"Of course, Marilyn," she replied, rolling the "r" in my name, making it sound exotic. She said she was a gypsy, but even being as young and innocent as I was, I had my doubts about that.

From then on, I read the palm of anyone who would allow me to do so. After I returned to Chicago, whenever I began my fortune telling routine, I was the hit of every party I attended.

During the rest of the year, I continued to study ballet with Edna McRae.

I worked hard and danced so many hours that at one point, my feet swelled to twice their size. But I never stopped. It was something that obsessed me.

Helen never really liked the fact that I was studying ballet. She preferred the glamorous look of showgirls and their slimmer legs rather than the more muscular look of ballerinas. But, as always, she remained supportive of my ambitions and dreams.

Even the most famous of dancers continue to practice, no matter where they find themselves. In every city they went to the major studios to remain in peak condition, and in Chicago, they came to Edna McRae.

One afternoon, members of the Joffrey Ballet visited the studio, and when I arrived, I sensed a flurry of excitement.

As the other students gushed with excitement, I became swept up with the idea that someone, anyone, from this prestigious dance company might watch me dance and discover my talents. But I had not prepared the way I should have, and Miss McRae, true to character, pulled me aside and taught me a lesson I shall never forget.

She slapped me. Hard.

"You missed your audition," she hissed. "Do you understand?"

I was stunned.

"Never, *ever,* come to my class unprepared or not at your best. Your leotards and tights were not new. Your hair was not styled properly. You destroyed your chance. You ruined an opportunity."

Stabbing her finger into my chest, she admonished, "In all your life, you may never get another chance like the one you just missed. *Do you understand?*"

I did.

I rode the el train home that night with my head bowed, not looking at anyone around me. I understood completely. Success is when opportunity meets preparation. Never again, I vowed, would I be ill-prepared in any situation.

There was always a brighter side to life and meeting Ken Beachler, a fellow student of Edna McRae and Everett Clark, was one of them. I had such a crush on him.

Ken was charming and never failed to make me laugh. Often, we would stop for a bite to eat after class and we became very close. His birthday was October 11 while mine was October 18, and we celebrated together as fellow Libras.

At the time, I believed myself to be madly in love with Ken and when he invited me to visit his family in Michigan one weekend, I was so excited. On a rainy Friday evening, I packed my things and Ken picked me up for our wonderful sojourn. Driving through the south side of Chicago, however, our plans were interrupted when his car stopped. Luckily, we found a gas station, where a mechanic informed us that the car's brakes needed to be replaced. There was nothing else to do but wait.

For whatever reason, I began to tap my feet as I paced the floor of the garage, and in short order, Ken followed suit. Before long, we were tapping out routines from class and a small crowd of people materialized to watch us. They burst into applause when we finished; it was one of those strange, memorable experiences I shall never forget.

He became a lifelong friend and to this day, we still laugh over practicing "Adagio," which required Ken to lift me over this head. At the time, he told Miss McRae that he had never lifted such a heavy girl in all his life, and continues to chide me over the fact that his doing so invoked a hernia.

I was never exposed to any African-Americans in my neighborhood while I was growing up, but I was also not exposed to prejudice either. When I first began my lessons with Edna, I excelled in tap dancing and she decided that I should take private lessons with Jimmy Payne, a famous black tap dancer, whose studio was located on South Wabash Avenue in Chicago.

"If you can develop the rhythm of a black dancer, I think you will become a better artist," Miss McRae explained. "You seem to have a natural ability to dance that way."

So I took lessons with Jimmy, who taught me triple wings and tacit tap, which is dancing without music. It was Jimmy who paid me one of the best compliments I ever received when he said, "You know, Marilyn, you have the rhythm and style of a black dancer."

Dance studios can be dreary places. They have mirrors, ballet barres, and wooden floors, with a few wooden or metal chairs placed in corners for visitors. It is the dancers who make the studio, and at Jimmy's studio, the dancing was exhilarating. I was constantly being challenged. Tap is not easy, and is full of tricky foot movements.

I became so good at dancing tap, Edna asked me teach it to her classes at the studio. This, of course, was the ultimate compliment this demanding woman could give me. No other student had ever before been asked to teach at Edna's studio.

As high school ended, I was only sixteen years old. I spent the next year with Edna McRae and found myself questioning whether to continue with dance and establish the career I had dreamed about or go to college. To Miss McRae, this should not have even been a question in my mind. Her life was dance, not academics.

It was Helen who insisted that I attend college. I really had no choice in the matter. She always won.

Despite my long hours at rehearsals and dance lessons, I maintained a high enough grade-point average to allow me to enter Northwestern University on a partial math scholarship.

In order to pay for additional tuition and books, however, I also needed to continue working.

Chicago's Chez Paree was one of the most famous night clubs on the Near North Side. Popular with both Chicagoans and tour-

My high school graduation photo

ists alike, it was widely known for its grand style, glamour, and entertainment, attracting the biggest headliners of the day.

When I was about twelve years old, my cousins' grandfather, Pat Mangan, visited Chicago on business. He invited Helen and me to join him for a special dinner and took us to the Chez Paree. I had never been inside a nightclub before and was in awe—looking at the beautifully set tables, the stage, the large band, and the candlelight.

After Pat danced with Helen, he asked me to dance. I'm sure that people looked at us thinking, "My goodness, she really has an interesting Sugar Daddy, doesn't she?"

I remember looking around that nightclub, watching the show, and thinking how absolutely marvelous it must have been to be a dancer in such a special place. How beautiful and glamorous the dancers seemed to me, and what fun they appeared to be having.

When word spread through Miss McRae's studio of openings in the chorus line at the Chez Paree, I knew that it could be a unique opportunity to dance while attending college. With Helen's encouragement, I made the decision to audition.

Needless to say, I was thrilled when I received not only the job, but a weekly salary of one-hundred twenty-five dollars, a very large amount of money at that time. It was if Helen knew all along that long slim legs were important, and that they would dance me into a good job.

Edna McRae, however, was not pleased at all.

She disparaged the very idea of my enrolling at Northwestern University. It made no difference to her what you thought—it was all about devoting your concentration to dance. What's more, to Edna, the idea of her protégée as a showgirl was a personal insult.

When I broke the news to her that I had become a Chez Paree Adorable, she slapped me hard across my face.

"I believed in you," she seethed. "I believed in your talent and now look at you and your utter disregard. I never want to see you again."

I was absolutely heartbroken and for the next twenty years, she refused to speak to me.

The Chez Paree was certainly nothing like Edna's dance studio. One week, it was Tony Bennett who performed, the next it was Nat King Cole. The atmosphere was terribly exciting and I was thrilled to have the wardrobe people custom fit me with rhinestones, sequins, and elaborate feathered headpieces and fans.

Upon opening night, I was so excited that I could think of little else. Just before we were to go on stage, a man approached, asking for my union dues.

Quite perplexed, I asked, "My what?"

"Your dues! Your union dues!" he demanded. "You owe one-hundred twenty-five dollars."

I didn't have that much money and said, "I'm sorry, I don't think that I wish to be a member of your union. I cannot afford it."

"You can't work here, if you don't belong to the union, honey," he snapped, tapping his foot impatiently.

Then I realized the gravity of my circumstances. Unless I was able to pay those dues, I would be unable to perform. My lack of funds was literally holding up the show. The band would not play. I didn't know what to do.

Donjo Levine, one of the Chez Paree's owners, caught wind of the situation and pulled me into his office.

I could feel my heart beating in my throat.

Backstage at the Chez Paree

"Listen, Marilyn," he said. "I'll advance you the money, but you'll have to pay it back. We'll deduct it from your pay." He wrote out a check, gave it to the union representative, and the show finally began.

Eventually, I did repay Donjo's loan in full, but I have never forgotten his act of kindness or any of the wonderful things that others have done for me since.

My life was not easy, but it was fulfilling.

During the day, I attended classes at Northwestern in the northern suburb of Evanston. Then I took the el train to Chicago's near north side, where the club was located.

We would rehearse, and then I would apply my elaborate makeup and costumes, stealing time to do my homework before and between each show. I danced until well after midnight and took two buses and another train home, napping until the bus drivers or conductor awakened me so that I could either transfer or exit. Helen stayed awake to greet me every night and always there was a hot, nourishing meal waiting for me on the table. Steak, mashed potatoes, carrots, and salad were my favorites.

One day, I was called into the manager's office.

Quietly he said, "Marilyn, I have been watching you. This club has an image to uphold and the school girl clothes you wear are unacceptable. As an 'Adorable,' you are expected to look the part when entering and leaving the club each night."

My wardrobe, he suggested in the nicest possible way, would have to be enhanced. I needed the job, and invested in more stylish clothes, paying closer attention to my image and appearance at all times.

Backstage with Tony Bennett

I was now living two lives.

I was a struggling co-ed, attending courses, rushing a soror-
ity, going to homecoming dances, and having deep discussions
over coffee with friends about the meaning of life and philosophy. I was also part of the glamorous world of the nightclub
circuit, dancing with the likes of Red Skelton, Nat King Cole,
Sammy Davis, Jr., Danny Kaye, and Tony Bennett.

The chorus line usually watched all of the headliners' rehearsals and I paid close attention to their dancing.

I asked Sammy Davis, Jr., his father Sammy, and Eddie Jackson to show me some of their steps, since I had never seen such
footwork. Most often we tapped to no music. The drummer
would beat out a rhythm and away we went. Da Da Dum! Da Da
Da Dum! Dada Da Dum! Dum! Dum! Often the musicians

With Sammy Davis, Jr.

would clap their hands to establish a beat and we would pound
out the same rhythm with our feet.

Ray Bolger was another wonderful performer, whose movements I carefully studied. Never was I too ashamed or bashful
to ask him or anyone else, for that matter, to teach me a step I
had observed.

One day at rehearsal I was watching him and he noticed my attempts to mimic one of his steps. "Come on up here with me," he said. "I'll show you."

And he did.

That masterful light step he had was the complete opposite of the "grounded to the earth" type of dancing I knew. Ray was much lighter on his feet, almost as if he were dancing on clouds and his technique was based on the "Highland" style.

The Chez Paree was a glorious place, where I was always given star-status. I loved watching the other girls receive flowers every night and hoped that one day someone would do the same for me. To my delight, one evening, an exquisite bouquet of red roses arrived with an accompanying card that read: "Love, Sammy." I was thrilled and although I had no idea who Sammy was, I met him after the show to thank him.

Gradually, he came to the Chez Paree every night to watch me dance, each time sending to me those glorious roses. One night, after speaking at length, Sammy said, "Please come with me, Marilyn. I would like to give you an entire room filled with flowers."

I was always leery of men and the idea of going anywhere with them, but he seemed like a nice gentleman and so I agreed to go out with him after my performance. As it turned out, he took me not for a late night dinner or a date, but to his flower shop! Aside from being quite relieved, I was overwhelmed when he unlocked the door to the store revealing the most beautiful flowers I had ever seen.

"You can have any of them or all of them," he said. "We'll put them in the car and I'll drive you home. Whatever you want."

Blushing, I leaned over to smell a fragrant blossom and felt something wet on my ear. "I like you so much, Marilyn," he whispered.

I nearly jumped out of my skin.

"I need to leave now, Sammy," I told him and did so without further delay. On the bus ride home that evening, I considered this experience to be a valuable lesson and was determined to be more careful in the future. There are no free roses in life.

Slowly, the balance between school and glamour became more and more unsettling. Performing on stage in full makeup and elaborate costumes, I became someone else. The applause, adulation, and excitement fulfilled me in a way that college did not. I was so busy working, that I found it difficult to concentrate in school with so little sleep. When you live a separate life at night, football homecomings are no longer important.

I attended Northwestern University for two years, but did not stay to receive my degree. How could I, when Jimmy Durante offered me a job in his troupe?

I had met him while he was performing at the Chez Paree.

With Jimmy, I would be making good money. I would travel the country and have the honor of working with one of the most famous and kindly entertainers of my generation.

Jimmy particularly liked tall girls with long legs, so that is probably why I was selected when I auditioned for him. This was an opportunity I could not pass up. After all, there was only one Jimmy Durante.

Jimmy's troupe was called Clayton, Jackson, and Durante. Sonny King worked with them when he was just starting out. I was one of five chorus girls who traveled with Jimmy, who was very protective of us. Never were we permitted to go anywhere unescorted.

At that time, musicians had a very dissolute reputation. When the band's trumpet player asked me out, I naively accepted. While dressing for my date, I received a phone call from Jimmy asking why I had not come downstairs for dinner.

"Oh, I'm not coming tonight. I have a date with Mike."

Backstage with Jimmy Durante

"Young lady," he announced, "*nobody* dates a trumpet player."

Jimmy abruptly canceled my date and I sheepishly joined the rest of the troupe for dinner that night.

One other thing that he wouldn't allow was for us to sunbathe. For that I shall always be grateful. As we now know, the sun ages the skin prematurely and can cause cancer.

Jimmy had a phobia about flying and so the whole troupe traveled with him by train. He always liked being surrounded by people and I often sat across from him on the train while he serenaded us with songs he made famous, including "Ink-A-Dink-A-Do."

Everywhere we went, doors opened for Jimmy Durante and his entourage.

One evening, in New Orleans, he took all of us to a strip-tease show on Bourbon Street starring Reddy Flame.

"I'm taking you to this place as a lesson," he said," so that none of you will ever be involved in this kind of performance."

Never before in my life had I witnessed anything like Miss Flame's performance. Needless to say, I never forgot Jimmy's eye-opening lesson.

I spent most of my salary on clothes, although I did manage to send some home for my family whenever possible. I only went on dates because I would be taken out to dinner. I learned how to say no to men without them ever realizing that I was doing so—a useful lesson in life for a young, single woman, especially at that time.

In one city, the hotel where we stayed happened to be hosting an entire football team. There we were, five young ladies amidst dozens of brawny young men. Naturally, we attracted their attention and as I was walking to my room, one of the largest men on the team followed me.

I turned into the hallway and he confronted me, putting his massive arms in front of me, pinning me next to the door.

"You're a very pretty girl," he said, "and I sure would like to be with you."

The man was as big as a truck. What does one do when a six-foot, four-inch body of solid muscle has you in his grip?

I ducked down and ran through his legs.

My agility surprised him, and I did not stop running until I came to a party down the hall.

I joined the group, finally feeling safe and when this young man came looking for me, I maintained my composure.

"Another time, perhaps," I demurred, all the while knowing that I would not be able to walk to my room alone while he still was in the hotel.

Traveling became quite lonely and the work was exhausting—three-hundred eighty-nine shows in nine months! I missed my mother and grandmother, who wanted me to be with them. Finally, I had to make a decision as to whether I should stay in show business, or rejoin my family.

I chose my family.

And so, I returned to Chicago, with my new makeup, well-coifed hair, and my beautiful clothes. A short time later, I was asked out on a date by a very well-known man. He took me to the Pump Room, famous for its celebrity clientele. When I commented on the lovely tablecloth, he snapped his fingers. The waiters removed all of the dishes and presented to me the linen so that I could take it home.

Innocently, I made another remark about the telephone on the table. Sure enough, that too was removed and presented to me.

Although I found it interesting to be with people who had such power, it did not impress me. I always knew who I was, and flattery and influence did not turn my head then or now. It has always been more important for me to be myself.

I choose to enjoy the company of others whose goals in life are more meaningful than ordering people around.

Even then, I knew that my dreams were important and could take me to a place where I could make a difference in the world.

Believing in dreams is essential.

To see the potential in life and in yourself is the basis for those dreams coming true. My cousin's grandmother, Leona Mangan, was a wealthy, beautiful woman and a Christian Scientist practitioner. She once told me, "You are your own help. You are your own person. There is a Godlike quality in all of us."

She was right.

CHAPTER TWO

Never stop dreaming, because dreams can become a reality.

When I left show business, I thought my background in theater would give me entry to a new life. I knew that if I wished to pursue my dancing career, it would require my moving to New York or to California. I wanted to stay in Chicago to be near my mother and grandmother, and so I decided to accept whatever jobs I was offered to allow me easier entrance into early television as a model.

At that time, Chicago was one of the main centers for television production and the industry was still in its infancy. I auditioned at a local station and landed my first job doing a commercial for Ford, dancing around an automobile. I was delighted to be dancing again, my hair pulled back and my feet turned out.

Meanwhile I paid close attention to the other models auditioning for television—they all had enormous eyes, glorious cheek bones, and were very poised, positioning their bodies in ways I was not used to. Their makeup was very different than my own, and their clothes were much more sophisticated.

I was determined to become a successful model. To make ends meet, I posed for hours on end for fashion sketch artists. Then I worked in the garment district on west Jackson Blvd., doing showroom modeling. There, I modeled raincoats in a small, stuffy showroom for twelve hours with no breaks.

The owner of the coat company was an unscrupulous character, who took one leering look at me and said, "Honey, you're the most flat-chested woman I have ever seen."

Needless to say, I did not hold those associated with the garment district in very high regard and eventually, I switched to convention modeling.

Shortly thereafter, I did a Dior show for Saks Fifth Avenue—an utterly glorious experience, because the fashion experts there were upset with my bra size. I could not believe that they found me to be too busty, since I was always a little self-conscious about what I considered my lack of curves. To my amazement, the show's fashion director actually wrapped my chest in tight scarves to make me look more flat-chested!

I did auto shows, boat shows, and furniture shows. Dressed in formal clothes and high heels, it was my job to speak knowledgably about the merchandise and to sell it, all the while smiling at the passers-by. It was made quite clear to me that the purpose of my presence was to attract attention for the product. This became the beginning for my sales training.

I carefully observed other models at my own auditions. Sometimes I was rejected, but once in a while, I was accepted. It was then I realized that Edna McRae was right—one needs to be prepared for every opportunity in order to succeed. The vocal coaching I had received from Everett Clark gave me an edge over other models and so I began auditioning for voice-overs.

Modeling for a boat show

From there I mustered the courage to do hand modeling where only one's hand is shown on screen or in a photograph, holding a bottle of detergent or showing off a diamond ring.

Finally I tried my luck in photo modeling and that was when I met resistance. "You don't have a *look*," I was told. Some photographers were kind enough to work with me and suggest, "Try this," or "Try that," but most could not be bothered with an inexperienced model.

I endured an endless string of "cattle calls," sitting in a room with dozens of other models around me. The person in charge, followed by his entourage, would quickly size up each woman and say either "good," or "leave." No one told you anything else, let alone the reason why you did not get the job.

I kept trying to develop my "look," the appearance that would set me apart from other models. This was, of course, quite difficult, because we rarely see ourselves as others see us. The people who ran the agencies and arranged the bookings for models were quite blunt about my shortcomings but not terribly helpful in sharing any suggestions as to how I might improve. Often times, they were rude. I sometimes believed that the agencies went out of their way to hire some of the most calculating, unfriendly people in the world.

What I failed to realize was that as a model, I was merely a commodity for sale. I took everything personally, which was not only foolish, but would hold me back from success.

Yet, I never gave up. Instead, I continued to make modeling rounds, calling on at least a half-dozen to a dozen photographers each and every day. It became perseverance, rejection, rejection, and perseverance. Many evenings I cried, wondering how long I could endure this humiliation.

More than anything else, I wanted to model for an exclusive store. The finest department stores in Chicago and other large cities had in-house models to showcase beautiful designer gowns and glorious international fashions to wealthy women, and to the men who were making purchases for their wives.

After being rejected at several fashion show auditions at Marshall Field's, I finally mustered enough courage to ask Gloria DeBais, then in charge of the models, why she had not hired me.

"Your makeup and hair are totally wrong," she said, looking me up and down. For the first time, someone had told me precisely what I needed to know. I finally understood that live modeling required a completely different look than the theater. Needless to say, I was quite devastated by Gloria's comments. I had always felt that I was quite knowledgable in matters of makeup and style given my theatrical background. I was learning the hard way that modeling and theater were worlds completely unrelated to one another and I was determined to take Gloria's advice to heart.

Rather than feeling sorry for myself, I decided, instead, that in order to develop a look all my own, I would first need to be re-educated at a modeling school. After all, what better place was there to learn? I certainly could not afford to take a two-thousand dollar course, so I applied for a job at Patricia Stevens, teaching ballet and fencing, which I had learned in physical education class at Northwestern University.

At Patricia Stevens, I began to sit in on makeup and hair-styling classes, as well as other courses in social graces, fashion runway, and photo modeling. I learned the techniques so quickly that I was asked to actually teach these classes. Abraham Lincoln once said, "If you understand it, you can then teach it," and I did.

At this time, I was also refining my wardrobe. I learned of the special places where professional models shopped, and carefully saved my money so I could purchase the accoutrements necessary for my new look. What I could not afford, my grandmother made for me.

Wherever I went, Helen also followed and shortly after I began working at Patricia Stevens, she began a part-time position there, as well.

When I began to obtain jobs, I carefully studied other models, noting exactly how they achieved unique effects with their

My first modeling composite

makeup. I knew that the more I learned, the more I would be successful in this newly chosen career.

Meanwhile, my good friends Peggy Fleischner and Rosie O'Neil planned a spring ski weekend in Michigan. I had never

49

Another promotional photograph

skied, but thought it might be an interesting experience. At the last minute, however, I received a modeling assignment, and since I needed the money, I canceled my weekend plans and went off to my job.

Part of an ad campaign for the Patricia Stevens school

Upon her return, Peggy kept talking about the nice man she had met named Lee Albert Miglin. He was so polite and such a gentleman that when her date became drunk and was unable to return her to the city, Al offered to drive her home. She saw him once or twice, but was really more interested in her hometown sweetheart, Ron Peterson.

When I first met my husband-to-be, he was waiting for Peggy in the lobby of the Patricia Stevens building at 22 West Madison, where we worked. He had the most wonderful demeanor and smile and I began talking to him while waiting for my own date to show up. Al was tall and dashing, with dark hair, glorious white teeth, and sparkling blue eyes. I must admit that I found him to be quite attractive.

When he called a week later to ask me out, however, I was absolutely horrified. He was, after all, Peggy's friend.

"How can you be so presumptuous?" I fumed. "I never date a friend's boyfriend." Then I added, "If you wish to date me, you must get Peggy's permission first." I was sure that would bring the matter to an end.

It was just the beginning.

Peggy confided to me, "I like Al. He is the consummate gentleman, Marilyn. But, you know that I really care about Ron, and I am hoping he will ask me to marry him when I go home to Minneapolis this summer.

"Why don't you just go out with Al Miglin once and see what happens?" she asked.

So I did.

Our first date was not exactly a disaster, but he did not impress me at all. He picked me up in a white Impala convertible with a red interior and took me to the Esquire Theater on Oak Street to see the movie *Five Pennies*. The theater was crowded and we had to sit in the balcony. The seats that high up were not designed with a tall, long-legged woman in mind, and as I sat with my knees practically under my chin, I thought, "What a lot of nerve this man has not to consider asking me if I even *wanted* to go to a movie."

I was used to a gentleman taking a lady to dinner on a first date, which Al did not do. Not only that, but when he took me home, he grabbed me and kissed me. I was horrified by his bad manners. I never allowed anyone to do this without my permission, especially on a first date. I got into my apartment, closed the door behind me and ran to the bathroom to wash my mouth out with Listerine. Who did he think he was?

I was angry, and fortunately for him, he did not phone for a week. I could think of nothing but getting even with him.

When he finally called, it took all his salesmanship to convince me that I should go out with him a second time. "Oh, indeed," I said through clenched teeth. "I would just love to," thinking that I would really do something to fix him.

On this second date, he took me to dinner and dancing under the stars at the Sheraton Hotel's Top of the Hat Restaurant. We had an absolutely wonderful evening and under the guise of getting to know him better, I read his palm.

Al was one of seven children—he was the middle child. His father had been a coal miner. Al enlisted at the age of seventeen and became a fighter pilot. Following the war, he utilized the GI Bill and enrolled in business college at the University of Illinois, working odd jobs to support himself. An extremely resourceful man, one summer he traveled across the country selling sunglasses from his car. Later, he sold Muntz televisions and pancake mix, fine-tuning his techniques in salesmanship.

Upon finishing college, Al had decided that one of three careers would make his fortune—insurance, oil, or real estate. Ultimately, he chose real estate and begged Abel Berland, executive vice president of Arthur Rubloff and Company, to give him a job. When Mr. Berland declined, Al said, "That's fine. You

A trip to an amusement park with Al

With Al (left) and my friend Ken Beachler, at the Indiana Dunes

don't have to pay me. Just let me make cold calls and you won't be sorry."

Listening to Al, I could not help but be dazzled by his sincerity, integrity, and charm. This time, when he took me home and kissed me good-night, I enjoyed it.

From that moment on, we saw each other every single night for the next three weeks.

During the fourth week, he regretfully told me he had to be out of town for a week, and I found myself missing him very much. When he returned, I was happy to see him and we resumed dating every single night. Our feelings for each other had become so passionate, that one evening neither of us could eat the elegant dinner the waiter placed before us. It was obvious that we had fallen in love and food didn't seem to matter.

Meanwhile, I had been offered a job as head of the Patricia Stevens school in San Francisco.

Six weeks from the day we met, Al invited me for dinner at the Italian Court Restaurant. After a few martinis and crepe suzettes with brandy for dessert, he presented to me the most exquisite marquise diamond engagement ring. He had closed a real estate deal and believing in nothing less than the best, had used his commission to purchase an absolutely perfect two-and-a-half-carat stone.

"Marilyn," he grinned, "will you marry me?" It was so gallant of him, but Al was a romantic.

I, on the other hand, did not know what to say. Of course I loved him, but there was also my career to consider.

"No, I will not marry you," I gently protested. "What about my new opportunity in San Francisco? Do you expect me to give up my career?

"I am also going to buy you a dining room set," he said to clinch the deal. I did not yet have a dining room, let alone an apartment to put furniture in, but ever the consummate businessman, Al wanted to make sure he had totally convinced me to marry him, and I was charmed.

How could I refuse?

To this day, I have never once regretted sacrificing my career opportunity at the Patricia Stevens west coast school in exchange for a dining room set.

We toasted our engagement with more wine and became quite giddy with excitement before leaving to celebrate further at the Pump Room, where we met several friends. There the martinis continued to flow. I was never much of a drinker, and so, in an inglorious end to a wonderful evening, I ended up passing out. Somehow, Al, who was in a slightly better state than I, packed me back into his car and drove me home. Then we both fell asleep in the car he had somehow managed to park in front of my apartment house.

My poor mother had to come out to retrieve us, but fortunately she saw the humorous side to the situation. When we were coherent enough to tell her the reason for our condition, she was delighted about our engagement, although for many years afterwards we heard a lot about the other aspects of that evening, including the fact that in order to sober me up, Helen had placed me in the bath tub filled with only a half inch of water, fearing that, in my condition, I would drown.

The next day, I visited the beauty shop and as I reclined my head into the shampoo bowl, my head was still spinning.

Although I had repeatedly questioned Al about his own family, he declined to introduce us until after we had become engaged, explaining later, "I wanted to make sure that you accepted me and not my family."

We drove to his home in Westville to visit the Miglin clan, who were both thrilled and amazed with the news. As Al was already thirty-five years old and had never before been married, they had lost hope that he would ever do so and were absolutely delighted at our engagement.

We were married six weeks later, on November 14, 1959 in Old Saint Mary's, at that time, the oldest church in Chicago. The Chinese priest who officiated, Father Fu, was an old friend, and he was so nervous he kept forgetting my name.

"Marilyn," Al kept on prompting him. "It's Marilyn."

I was so frightened of taking such a big step. What if it didn't work? Where would I go? On the last night that I spent with Helen at home, she said, "I never expect to see you at my home again without your husband. Even if you have doubts about your marriage over the years, you must talk through any of your problems. That means you do not run home to me. You must work out any problems together."

Ever the chivalrous gentleman, Al exclaimed that if I was changing my own name by taking the last name Miglin, it was only fair that he should change his as well. Given his grand aspirations for success, we decided that "Lee," his real first name, was a much more formidable moniker for a future real estate tycoon.

And so it was, that Marilyn Janice Klecka became Marilyn Miglin and that Lee Albert Miglin became Lee Miglin.

Since we could not afford both a wedding and a honeymoon, we decided to use the money Lee made when he closed another real estate deal toward the security deposit and first month's rent for an apartment and a romantic honeymoon trip to Europe.

That is also why I never wore a wedding ring. There wasn't enough money for both the ring and a honeymoon. Over the years, if we were asked about the fact I wore only an engagement ring, Lee would say, "Without an official wedding ring, I

Our wedding picture

will always be engaged to the most wonderful woman in the world."

The first stop on our honeymoon was Germany. Lee was an accomplished skier, and there we purchased beautiful ski clothes, outfitting me in an all-white ensemble with white boots. We also purchased our first silver flatware.

Packing all of our beautiful sweaters, pants and newly acquired treasures into a little Volkswagon we had driven from Stuttgart, we set off for London and then Paris, before driving to the south of France.

We arrived on a cool, crisp November evening and after checking into the Negresco Hotel in Nice, we dressed in formal attire and walked to an elegant casino. I must admit that I was very nervous about being there. Gambling was certainly not legal in Chicago, but colorful stories about the underground world there, filled with characters such as "Little Anthony" and "Tommy the Fin" abounded. My own naivete fueled my growing trepidation just standing there watching the dealers and the players.

Lee, on the other hand, had already traveled throughout Europe and was quite worldly. Dashing in his regalia, he whisked me through the casino to the blackjack tables. "No, no, no!" I protested. "You cannot gamble, Lee. This is dangerous."

"Trust me," he insisted. And with that, he won the first hand. And then he won his second hand. Then the third and a fourth. I watched nervously, my eyes darting about, just waiting for someone to push through the crowd and drag him away.

When he finally stopped, he had won over one-hundred dollars—quite a tidy sum of money in those days. He cashed out and as we left the casino, I was just sure that we were being followed by large men in pinstripe suits with big guns who wanted to recoup their money.

We used the money to pay for our first magnificent dinner on the French Riviera. The fact that the weather changed that night and that it began to rain did not matter to us. It was an exciting and romantic evening.

The next morning, conditions had become increasingly stormy. On my way to a very chic beauty salon in the hotel, I noticed that the waves outside were increasingly high, but didn't give it another thought. In the salon, I was pampered and polished from head to toe, and I was enjoying every moment.

As my hair was being combed, however, there was suddenly a great flurry of excitement in the salon. I swiveled in my chair, to see customers and salon technicians rushing about with decided urgency and as I was unable to speak French fluently at the time, I was not fully aware of what was happening.

Curiously, some employees began stuffing towels under the doors, while others rushed in with sandbags.

"Madame, si'l vous plait," the beautician said, almost in tears. "I have to leave for a moment."

I waited, but she did not return.

When I finally realized that no one was going to finish my hair or manicure, I left the salon to look for Lee. Meanwhile, the Negresco staff began barricading the entire hotel with boards.

Then the electricity went off.

Moments later, Lee came running in to find me, after having moved the car a mile away to protect our valuables—all of the beautiful things we had purchased throughout our trip.

What we had finally managed to decipher was that a huge tidal wave was quickly approaching. We rushed upstairs to our room and sat in total quiet and darkness. It was a very romantic setting for newlyweds who didn't have the sense to realize the danger they were in. For the next three days, we were hotel-bound in the south of France with meals by candlelight and no outside communication. It may not have been the best of times for the locals, but for us it was the perfect ending to a wonderful honeymoon.

Upon finishing our travels in Europe, we had only ninety-six dollars between us and no savings awaiting us at home. We did have some wonderful clothes and Christmas gifts, and of course, our new silverware. I only hoped that we would not be stopped at customs upon our return to Chicago, as we would have been unable to pay the debts incurred by any duties owed. Fortunately, however, we sailed through.

When we returned home, we were startled to discover one of Lee's bachelor buddies waiting for us at our new apartment. It seemed that he missed Lee and was without a place to stay. What were we to do? My first two weeks as a new bride were spent entertaining our house guest.

Lee continued to establish himself in real estate and I continued to model. Our first apartment was at 30 East Elm, and I decorated it in every shade of purple imaginable. It was very dramatic and I felt exhilarated furnishing our new home.

We loved having parties and had a natural ability as hosts. I have never believed in asking someone to bring anything to a party. If you invite them into your home, it is your obligation to entertain them, and with my European heritage, I was taught to prepare more food than necessary. Do it well, or do not do it at all.

It was at one of our gatherings that I met Dorsey Conners, who became one of my best friends. John Forbes, whom she later married, brought her to our house as his date. Through the years, the four of us shared much in our lives, celebrating together the good, and consoling each other through the bad times.

Shortly after we established our new home, my grandmother, whom I admired and loved, retired. She was a very straightforward, elegant woman, perfectly dressed and immaculately groomed. She always wore a smile, but she never accepted a woman laughing loudly ,or making a spectacle of herself. Every Friday, on my day off, I picked her up and brought her to my

Mr. and Mrs. Lee Miglin

apartment, where we spent the entire day together doing laundry, cleaning, and baking bread. Despite our closeness, there were times when she would become quite angry with me and argumentative, like Helen. But through her wisdom and criticism, I learned a great many things.

Lee was terribly distraught over where she lived—a tiny apartment overlooking an alley. My Aunt Virge lived in a three-flat walk-up building and now that I had married, Helen was completely alone.

After discussing the situation, we decided it was necessary to ensure that our families were well taken care of before establishing our own goals and priorities. Together, we scrimped and saved in order to purchase a three-flat building, where each of my family could enjoy her own apartment while remaining close together. Six months after our wedding, Lee put down a deposit on a beautiful building on Lorel Avenue near Fullerton. My grandmother moved into the first floor, Helen had the second floor, and Virge took the third.

As I continued to teach at Patricia Stevens modeling school, Lee suggested that I enroll in their training program on the art of salesmanship.

In order to generate leads on prospective students, I learned to make cold calls, which I absolutely hated. When a young girl and her mother did visit the agency, they were never to leave without the girl being signed up for a two-thousand dollar course.

I took mothers and daughters on tours of the school, introducing them with great excitement to all of the glamorous teachers and their students, and when we returned to my office, I had to close the deal.

If the mother hesitated, answering, "I'll have to think about it," the response was, "What is there to think about? Your daughter has such potential. She'll take this invaluable education with her the rest of her life."

I was taught to work toward my objective and make the sale. Lee had insisted that this knowledge would be good for me, and indeed, in retrospect, it was.

Meanwhile, as a young real estate wife, I accompanied Lee to a convention of industrial brokers. I found it rather curious that the corporate wives I met at the hotel were quite visibly concerned about their makeup for a Saturday evening dinner we were to attend. How interesting it was, I thought, that these women who had been married for many years, with the means to live life to its fullest, were becoming so unraveled over who would apply their makeup when they were away from home.

Gradually, I built my own modeling assignments to the point that I felt confidant about leaving Patricia Stevens in order to concentrate fully on my career. In addition to modeling for Marshall Field's 28 Shop, Saks Fifth Avenue, Blum's Vogue, and The Pump Room. I was becoming one of the most sought after professional models in Chicago.

Modeling was all about improving and maintaining one's individual "look." Whatever it took to look our most glamorous was what we sought and it was not at all unusual to send all over the world for some bottle or pot of cosmetics we thought would make us look more divine on the runway.

In the fall of 1962, Lee's high sales won us a vacation to New York. A number of my friends, who knew about our trip asked that I purchase for them specialized beauty items that were available only there. "Could you just pick this up for me?" they asked. Before we left Chicago, I had twenty different orders from my friends for products we all thought were fabulous.

And so one Saturday in 1962, Lee and I looked in the New York telephone directory for addresses of stores where we could purchase these products. Interestingly, there were sixty-five cosmetics shops listed at that time in New York. The amazing fact was that we did not have *any* in Chicago. We had department stores and drug stores, but there were no makeup salons where one could purchase professional quality products.

Returning to Chicago, I could not stop thinking about such an obvious unfulfilled niche. It was time to think about the next phase of my life, as I knew that I could not continue to successfully model forever. At one point, I had considered opening a dance studio, but as I reflected more and more about both the unavailability of specialty cosmetic products in my own city, I became increasingly certain that there was a definite market demand. If my modeling friends appreciated these beautiful products, I reasoned, the average woman would enjoy them as well.

As my modeling assignments slowed down after the Christmas holidays, I discussed with Lee, the idea of opening my own business. Given the fact that I was so knowledgeable about makeup techniques, it seemed a logical thought.

"It's a good idea," he said, "but either do it or don't discuss it. No excuses allowed."

His response startled me, as I really wished only to discuss the possibility. I was not prepared for someone to actually tell me to just do it. Lee's philosophy, however, was that if you have a dream, you should pursue it and his comment served only to reinforce what I already knew to be true.

If it didn't work, at least I would have tried. I truly believe that people should never say, "If only. . .", "I should have. . .", or "If I didn't have a baby, I would have. . . ."

If you are to live your dream to its fullest, one must not make excuses, never blame others, and assume the responsibility for your own life. Do not ask permission for living. There is too much to do, too much to see, and so much to accomplish.

Shortly thereafter, I visited my modeling agency, A-Plus, on Oak Street to inquire as to any available modeling assignments and left my car with Luther, the valet. When I returned, I asked him, "Do you know of any spaces on Oak Street that might be available for rent?"

"Yes," he answered. "There's a little place upstairs over there at 110 East Oak," he said pointing across the street. "It's above a mail order cosmetics and vitamin house called Jean Farrell."

I hurried across the street to take a look and discovered that interestingly enough, the building also housed a fashionable resale shop called Entre Nous, owned by Mary Ann Ryan, a beautiful model whom I greatly admired. If Mary Ann could run a successful business, why couldn't I? Furthermore, her store was located at the rear of the building. Mary Ann's customers—both models and the most fashionable women in the city—would have to pass by the available space to reach her store at the end of the hallway. Perhaps I could attract some of her clientele as my own.

I made my decision, but had to convince the owner of the building that I would not be in competition with his mail order business, which was not an easy task.

Signing that lease was frightening, because I knew that there was no turning back. The rent was $250 a month for 500 square feet of space on the mezzanine floor of the building with a little balcony. We scraped together the security deposit and first month's rent, then Lee, Helen, and I painted the entire store pink. I hung all of my theatrical pictures along with those of my friends, purchased two used showcases and filled them with my tiny bottles of product.

I sent over seven-hundred letters to the companies who manufactured the types of makeup I sought, but only one-hundred forty-three answered. It was with those cosmetics that I began my business.

One day, a Max Factor salesman came in to visit me. I had wanted to carry Max Factor in my store, but the minimum opening order of two-thousand dollars prohibited me from doing so.

"You're not going to be successful," he said scornfully. "You'll be out of business in a week. Do you know that Muskett and Hendrickson, across the street, does sixty-four thousand dollars a year in cosmetic sales? Just how do you expect to compete?"

I was discouraged by his words, but not yet ready to give up.

I told all the models I knew about the shop and then sent handwritten letters to my friends inviting them to my opening party. The following morning, June 8, 1963, I officially opened my boutique for business.

At 10:30 a.m., a woman walking toward Mary Ann Ryan's resale shop stopped in and said, "Do you have a green eye shadow?"

I was so nervous that at first I didn't know where to find the item. And then, in one of those inspired moments that are such an important part of every person's life, I applied the shadow to one of her eyes and taught her how to do the other eye herself. That became the philosophy of my business, and still is today: that every woman learns to apply her own makeup in a way that is both correct and comfortable for her individual lifestyle.

No woman should be dependent upon someone else to apply her makeup properly, no matter where she is in the world. Looking her best is what makes a woman feel special about herself, and knowing the proper way to utilize cosmetics gives her an independence that is important for her self esteem. I knew that I could empower women by giving them new confidence. The women who visited me in my salon did not know how to use cosmetics, and they lacked confidence in their own judgment.

What I taught them is that good skin care comes from proper cleansing, priming, and hydration. I instructed my clients as to how they could use color to sculpt, contour and enhance their most positive features.

It is every woman's birthright to look and feel beautiful. When we look good, we feel good.

Those first few weeks of business, I worried constantly. I knew exactly how much I had to make to pay the rent, electric, and telephone bills—sixty-five dollars a day. This goal became my mantra.

On July 3, I had not had a customer all day, and I became concerned and nervous. At three in the afternoon, a young model, whose name I shall never forget, Mary Ann Anjelica, came in and made a three-hundred dollar purchase. This was a

My first shop on Oak Street

milestone for me, and Lee and I went away for the weekend to celebrate the fact there had not been a single day since opening my salon that I had not had a customer.

Before long, daily sales began to exceed two hundred dollars, and soon four hundred dollars. Continuing to model afforded me the unique opportunity of not needing to draw a salary from my own profits. I reinvested that money back into the salon.

When I had a booking, I would ask one of my model friends to watch the store. I was lucky, because these same friends would order cosmetics while they were there and other models would order from me during the shows that we worked together.

Word of mouth continued to spread.

One day, Peg Zwecker, a local columnist who was covering the Designer Import Show at Marshall Field's where I was modeling, asked what I had been doing and I told her about the salon. She wrote a column item about my store and women who were not in modeling suddenly learned that there was now a place in Chicago where they could purchase specialized cosmetics, beautiful false eyelashes, and also learn to apply makeup properly. Certainly, the best advertisement any business may obtain is the kind that requires no payment. That is the kind of publicity that consumers instinctively trust.

At the end of my first year in business, I needed help at the store. I was now able to pay a salary and so Helen, who was still working at Patricia Stevens, joined me at the salon. There were times that Helen did not agree with what I was doing, and there were days when she criticized me publicly. There were even days when she wouldn't speak to me at all. But she helped me build my business and still works with me to this day.

Not long after I hired Helen, one of my customers expressed her admiration for what I was doing and became my second employee. She was a wealthy woman with amazing style and glamour. One day, however, she announced that she wished to become my partner.

"Well," I hesitated, unable to find the exact words to express to her in a polite manner that I did not share the same desire. "I had not thought about the possibility of engaging a partner," I said. "I shall consider it and discuss it with Lee."

"You're so successful," she enthused, "I want to be a part of what you're doing."

Naturally, I did not wish to hurt her feelings, but I most definitely did not want to debate or discuss my business decisions or the manner in which I ran my shop with anyone else who had the power of a veto. Certainly, I could have grown much faster as a business with the money her partnership would have afforded. But with her came the baggage of her husband, who, shall I say, was a "slick businessman," quite persuasive in his demeanor and the manner in which he conducted his affairs. The more I reflected upon any possibility of a partnership and his subtle participation behind the scenes, the more I began to perceive the whole idea as a threat.

Lee and I both agreed that it would be unwise to acquire a partner and the next morning, when I declined her request, she threatened to sue me. On what basis, I was not quite sure. It did not matter. The whole incident left me ridden with angst.

I continued to work early in the morning doing fashion shows, returning to the salon during the day. Then it was back to the runway for evening shows as well. With an all-consuming passion to succeed, I never hesitated to reopen my door as I was closing for one more customer. It did not matter what I was doing or how badly I wanted to go home after an exhausting day. The customer always came first.

As my reputation among professional circles began to grow, Lee and I began visiting New York twice a year on "buying" missions, searching every neighborhood store for new and unusual products to sell at my salon.

My customers gave me the greatest education I could ever receive. I worked tirelessly with each and every woman who visited the store. The most challenging customers became my most loyal and I became known for making women feel more beautiful and glamorous than they ever thought they could be.

Every day, on the way to work, I passed a building next door to my shop that displayed a "for sale" sign. It was a grand, elegant old building with French architecture similar to places one might see on Rue St. Honorée in Paris. The woman who owned it, Ethel Doll, had run a couture dress salon and millinery shop on the first floor. She had died a number of years before and as her estate was still unsettled, the place was in terrible condition. Still, I loved its elegance, and each time that I passed it, I dreamed about owning it.

One day I mustered the courage to call the number on the sign and made an appointment to see the building. Lee accompanied me, and after we viewed it, said, "If you want to buy it, you will have to go to the bank and arrange for a mortgage."

So I put on my hat and gloves and scheduled an appointment with Lake Shore Bank, which managed Ethel's estate.

They asked, "What kind of collateral do you have?"

"I will have the building," I replied.

"No, no," they said. "We need more than that."

"But, you have had the building for over two years and not been able to sell it."

"Are you married? Do you have a husband? Does he have collateral?"

This was the way business was done in those days, especially for women, and I was naive in believing that I could obtain a mortgage on my own. The phone company worked with me, begrudgingly to open an account, but the gas company would not even consider putting my own name on the bill. Today, I still derive a mischievous enjoyment in ceremoniously tearing the gas out of any property I acquire.

If I were beginning my business now, things would be much different, but at that time, women starting a business had a difficult time obtaining financing, let alone basic amenities.

Fortunately, Lee was able to obtain the two mortgages necessary, and upon acquiring the building, we painted the walls soft pink to match the first salon. I rented out the basement and second floor, which helped pay the mortgages, and created a beautiful apartment on the third floor of the building for Helen.

Around that time, I began to think more and more about owning my own home. Our second "purple" apartment at 1550 Lake Shore Drive was lovely, but all my life I had lived in apartments, always very high up. I longed for a real home—a *house*.

My real estate husband suggested that I begin keeping a detailed record of available properties and visit each of them. Determined to find something both suitable and affordable, I set out to find our home. I carefully compiled notes for each property I saw, including information on square footage, the cost of utilities, taxes, and income. Each day, I visited another neighborhood to tour yet another house and before long, I had over two-hundred available properties duly recorded in my notebook.

For every property I felt appropriate, Lee made an offer, but it was always so low that it was never accepted. After sixty-five offers were met with sixty-five rejections, I found myself at wit's end.

One day, I found a beautiful house with a circular staircase and the most exquisite cove molding in the living room I had ever seen. Some of the roof had collapsed through the third floor, down through the second floor, and into the kitchen. The hearth was in shambles, but the property was a diamond in the rough. Lee acquired the keys for a weekend and after numerous walk-throughs, we expressed a mutual love for the property.

"Yes, it sure would be nice," he sighed.

I was furious.

"This is it," I told Lee. "I don't think you have been at all serious about purchasing a house. You've just been baiting me by keeping me busy and doing all of the work in finding a property. If you don't buy this house," I threatened, "then perhaps it's time to end our lives together."

Regarding my outburst with wide-eyed surprise, he finally understood that I was quite serious. It was my anger and frustration that pushed him to the next level.

Any employee of legendary real estate magnate Arthur Rubloff, for whom Lee worked, was assumed to be earning a great deal of money. And since the owner of the house happened to be an acquaintance of Mr. Rubloff's, we thought it wise to make an initial offer of twenty-thousand seventy-five-hundred dollars under Helen's name.

To my absolute delight, the offer was accepted.

The house was a mess. We moved into one of the rooms on the third floor while seventeen tradesmen stomped in and out of the bottom floors, hammering, plastering, and generally creating chaos. This was still a time in our lives that we had no money, and sometimes cutting corners to save a few dollars worked against us.

The architect who drew the plans for the house tried to keep his costs down, and somehow left the kitchen out of the blueprints. I finally found a carpenter who did a drawing of the whole house on a paper bag, including the kitchen. His name was Charlie Engel, a former Navy ship builder, and he became the man who transformed our house into a home. Lee and I adored him.

I suddenly found myself acting as the general contractor. Increasingly frustrated over the lack of professionalism of the electrician, who was always late, if he showed up for work at all, I finally reached my limit of tolerance. One day, I fired him.

"You can't fire the electrician!" the other tradesman told me.

"I can and I have," I replied, attempting to retain my composure, while not revealing that I had never before remodeled a house. Instead, I learned first hand about construction. Lee tore down walls, while Helen and I carried plaster to the dumpster in garbage bags and buckets.

Nine months later, we finally had a kitchen and a house.

While living in our apartment building, a neighbor had introduced me to a wonderfully talented interior decorator named Harold Walsh. I had been completely enamored with his work on their nine-room unit and wanted desperately to work with him on our home. Perhaps it was my passion, or maybe it was my smile. For whatever reason, he exclaimed, "Oh, I'd love to work with you! You have no money and you're so poor," he continued, rubbing his hands together in delight, "We'll have to do something on a shoestring budget and show everyone else that it can be done. This will be fun!"

I was not sure whether I should be humiliated or honored. Either way, work with me he did, and from Harold I learned a great deal about interior design and decoration. Because I was still modeling at Marshall Field's, I received a twenty percent discount off any purchase I made there. This became our means for decorating our new residence with elegance and style.

I continued modeling to pay the rent and expenses that the shop income did not cover. Most of my modeling assignments were screened quite carefully by my agency. One day, however, I received a call apprising me of a man looking for a tall, blonde model. He needed someone in a photo shoot for a name brand mattress.

During my dinner hour, while working as a house model in the 28 Shop at Marshall Field's, I went to a big warehouse on Lake Street where I had been instructed to meet the photographer. I took a freight elevator upstairs and introduced myself to the man who was setting up his cameras.

"Oh, you're just lovely! Why don't you change into this gown, and come back out here," he said, thrusting a peignoir set at me.

"But, why do I have to change?" I asked. "You can see how I look. I'll just sit near the bed."

"Oh, no," he purred. "I thought we could engage in some interesting conversation so I can learn more about your personality. That way, I can catch the true you on film."

I looked at him and then around the warehouse, suddenly realizing that the whole place was filled with nothing but beds and mattresses.

With a quick glance, I located the exit sign. I began backing away from him as he edged closer and closer to me.

"No, I don't think so. You've seen enough," I managed to say calmly. "I'm on my dinner hour and I have to get back to Marshall Field's. Why don't you give the agency a call."

I kept backing up, praying that I would not fall over onto a mattress. I made my way through the aisles, keeping a wary eye on him until I found the stairs, and began running down them as quickly as I could. He came after me, but I had a head start. Thankfully, the exit door was not locked and I sprinted to the car, where Lee was waiting.

"Let's go!" I shouted.

Lee started the car and away we drove. Only then did I explain what had transpired upstairs.

Photographers were always very coy. They always wanted to know "a little more about you." As a model, I always knew what I had to do, however, and learned to say "no" without ever actually saying it. No man ever recognized that I had subtly declined his advances and gained control of the situation. That, in itself, is an art-form.

I must have inherited from my paternal grandmother, the inclination to collect real estate. Somehow, she saved enough from her weekly grocery money to purchase her house as well as the one next door to her. Somewhere along the line, whether it was Lee's influence or some inherent personality trait passed down to me by my grandmother, a desire within me was awakened to follow her tradition of acquiring property.

One day, shortly after settling into our new house, we looked out into the yard across the way which was severely neglected. Judith Fitzpatrick, a friend of ours, had just become a real estate agent. We asked her to find out if the apartment building was for sale. Sure enough, she informed us that the elderly man who owned it was willing to sell.

We bought the property for a small amount down, obtained a mortgage, and ended up owning those four apartments, which we then rented. I managed the building for thirty-two years until we remodeled it into a single-family residence.

Later, I noticed a building across the street from us, which was also neglected by its owners. It seems that most of the buildings I have purchased have been in similar condition.

The owner asked me if I liked her building.

"I love it, but I cannot afford it," I said.

"Don't worry. I'll sell it to you for no money down," she replied.

When Lee came home from the office that evening, I said, "Darling, how would you like to buy a new building for no money down?"

Lee handled the negotiations, and in the end, I remember he bought this grand old lady of a house for only $100,000. This became another wonderful investment, and I managed that building as well as others we bought later.

It was very important for us to keep the neighborhood where we lived from decaying as other older areas in big cities often did. We began purchasing additional properties, remodeling or upgrading them, and then rented them, carefully selecting tenants who cared as much as we did.

The salon, meanwhile, became a place like no other—where models could work for a few hours a day and then return to the runway. This was my life as well. I was constantly running in and out in between modeling jobs. Everyone in the salon, my staff and the customers, were always in the limelight, and that brought a certain cache to the salon.

The women who worked for me became known as the "Miglin Beauties." They were recognized by their special look. Their makeup and mannerisms made them stand out from others. I emphasized to them when they were hired that no matter where they were, they must present not only the best of themselves, but my philosophy of real beauty coming from within.

The Beauties never took lunch in public. Our customers did not expect to see them eating—ignoring reality, and believing that was how models maintained their size eight figures. You might recall that in the movies of that time, no one ever ate. No beverages were ever poured—a full glass just miraculously appeared. No one in a Hollywood production ever said, "Excuse me, I have to go to the ladies room." We tried to maintain that same movie-star image of perfection in the salon.

During the 1960s, women bought a supply of eyelashes each time they came into the store, often times enough to last them for an entire year. False eyelashes were as hot then as ear piercing is now. I became known as the "Eyelash Queen of Chicago." Each lash was hand cut and hand fitted. Properly trimming one pair could take over an hour. The amount of time spent in demonstrating and assisting any one woman who was trying on eye-lashes is by today's standards, staggering.

My Beauties and I taught women who had never before pur-chased false lashes to wear them properly—by giving them a sheet of instructions and our personalized advice. Customers practiced applying them over and over again, and were not al-lowed to leave the shop until they had mastered the technique, not unlike learning how to wear contact lenses today.

It was necessary to ensure that they were applied properly to avoid an errant lash from falling into the soup course. Women would then return to share their stories: "I need a new left lash. It fell off in my champagne."

We replaced lashes lost to the predatory instincts of the fam-ily cat who had mistaken them for a spider and to a pet parakeet who decided they were a tasty bug. One customer always put her lashes in water before going to bed, and one night she drank them.

Every day, we received panicked calls from customers who absolutely *had* to have their lashes within minutes. It was an-other era.

One day, Musket and Henderson, the pharmacy down the street, caught fire amid dangerously high winds. Firemen posi-tioned themselves up and down Oak Street as a precautionary measure against the fire spreading. They were in front of my store and warned me to prepare for immediate evacuation at any given moment. Meanwhile, the phone was ringing off the hook with hysterical women who pleaded, "Please don't leave! I need my eyelashes."

One of my Beauties told a customer on the phone, "Mrs. Golding, there is a fireman standing outside who has threat-ened to pick me up and carry me out himself."

"Then just make sure to take my lashes with you!" she de-manded.

As a woman business owner in those days, I suppose that I was a pioneer. I would have faced the same problems had I owned a tire shop. The fact that my forte was the beauty business made no difference. At that time, the entire cosmetics industry was run by men—Revlon, Estee Lauder, and Max Factor were all controlled by male CEOs. When my business first opened, people assumed that my company as well was run by a man. Customers who came into the salon looked, not so subtly, over my shoulder for the male owner they were so sure was lurking in the background.

Product shipments arrived several times a week via tailgate delivery, meaning that the driver would only let down the back gate of a truck for unloading and do nothing else to assist. We had no strong man in the shop to unload these shipments. Drivers would ask for a signature to confirm delivery and would then proceed to scratch their heads when they saw only myself. I would simply analyze the size of the order and call back to the salon, "This will take at least four of us!"

Four of my Beauties would emerge and we would form a female chain to unload and stock merchandise. There were a few drivers who were polite enough to offer their assistance, but for the most part, the attitude I encountered was, "Look, lady! If you really want this shipment, then *you* take delivery!" Some of them would not even bother to open a door. We did it all ourselves—in high heels and mini-skirts, no less.

I was very happy with my new life. I was modeling on runways, doing photo-shoots, I had all of my beautiful little products and my business was flourishing. One day, however, I was startled to notice a consistent and steady stream of customers returning an undercover product I had been ordering from New York. Customers were telling me that the product was balling up around their eyes. They didn't like the undercover anymore and wanted their money back. Perplexed, I called the manufacturer and asked if he had altered the formulation.

"I haven't changed a thing with that product," he said in a tone indicating he would not tolerate my inquiry or complaints. "There's nothing wrong with it." End of conversation.

Obviously, however, there was something wrong, especially since, when I was applying makeup to models before shows, I noticed that the product was creasing in the fine lines around their eyes, something it had not done before.

Frustrated, Lee and I returned to New York and began an arduous search for a cosmetic chemist. There we followed every lead, walking, traveling by taxi, riding the subways, and venturing into strange neighborhoods in Brooklyn, the Bronx, and Harlem—wherever someone told us about a chemist who might work with us to evaluate this product. No one would even speak to us because I was ordering only a dozen pieces of product at a time rather than the two-thousand to five-thousand units they expected. I felt utterly dejected and discouraged.

Finally, a woman filling in for a receptionist at Strand Cosmetics in Brooklyn took pity on us. Her name was Sylvia Fiedler.

"My husband always likes a good challenge," she said. "I'll tell you what. You have such a sincere smile, I'll call him and you can talk to him."

Sylvia led us up a flight of creaky old stairs to her husband's laboratory, a fascinating place filled with beakers, raw ingredients, incubators, test tubes, and presses. Dr. George Fiedler was a cantankerous man with a balding head and thick glasses. He would later become a very special friend, but at that moment, he was not overly cordial.

In my hands, I held both an original product and the new undercover. "Dr. Fiedler," I pleaded, "You've got to help me. The manufacturer tells me that this is the same product they used to sell, but I don't think it is. Would you evaluate these to determine if they made any changes?"

"Well, I don't know," he huffed. "How many of these do you want to order from us if any changes have been made?"

"Maybe five or six dozen," I said.

"Why that doesn't even pay to begin evaluating it," he snapped. "But, I'll tell you what. I don't like this manufacturer. He isn't honest with his clients and so I'll check this for you."

He took the product into his lab and when he returned with the results, he was quite animated and obviously irate. "This is not the same," he seethed. "I despise charlatans! They're cheating you! No doubt about it," he continued, "but I can reformulate this and make it even better."

Dr. Fiedler's minimum order was two-thousand pieces, rather than the sixty I could afford. But I went out on a limb again, realizing that this makeup would become my own formulation. I found a white, round container with an opaque top and had my name hot stamped on to it. This was how I began my own line of cosmetics. There was no business plan, just a need to be in control of my own life and succeed in what I was doing.

Thus, my own products were derived from experimenting with the best cosmetics available, thereby perfecting them for my own formulations. I then began investigating laboratories that would work with me to make other products to my specifications.

At a lab in New Jersey, I met Charlie Marlowe, a world-renowned cosmetic chemist, who enthusiastically told me, "You're going to make it in this business!" The empowerment of that statement was so important to me that to this day, I continue to work with that laboratory, although it is now owned by Charlie's nephew, Mike Assante.

My second product was a powder that, without creasing or fading, set and held a woman's eye shadow color all day long until it was removed. As this was a "model secret" for maintaining eye makeup under the hot lights during long days of photo shoots and fashion shows, I called it *Modelite,* and it was Charlie's lab that produced it for me. Today, it remains my best-selling product.

At first, with my lack of knowledge about the manufacturing of makeup, I naively assumed that everything came out of production in one piece. I never stopped to consider the various components such as lids, bands, bases, and labels. Powdered makeup such as eye shadows and blush were pressed at a specific pressure point into a pan, glued into a base, and then affixed with a label. My first product was comprised of nine pieces.

Business continued to flourish and before long, I had expanded to five other locations in the Chicagoland area. I evolved step-by-step, arduously creating the most exquisitely beautiful products, incorporating my own packaging, until at last I had established a Marilyn Miglin Model Makeup line with twenty-five products.

Next, I ventured into the development of my own skin care products, each of them formulated to my exacting specifications. Since I handled my own purchasing, I planned my first skin care promotion for July 1, ordering products, which included one thousand pounds of toner to be delivered to my salon well in advance of the sale date.

Lee helped me design the sale postcards and I enjoyed a wonderful response to the mailing. I had my dates, I had sent my invitations, I had everything prepared . . . and then the delivery truck missed Chicago, continuing on to California. By the time my toner was found, it was ruined. I had to begin again with a new batch. I missed my sale date and had to back order, which meant lost time, lost revenue, and hundreds of letters of apology in addition to the cost of postage.

What did this disaster teach me?

It made me realize that I needed to create my own laboratory and take another crucial step in realizing the potential of my business. I was determined to take charge and not depend upon anyone else.

CHAPTER THREE

"To leave the world a little bit better than you found it, to know that one person's life is happier because of something you have done, and, most importantly, to gain the respect of your own children, is to be truly successful in life."

$\mathcal{L}$ee was fast becoming the most respected real estate developer in Chicago. My business was growing and our home was complete. My family was well taken care of.

It was time.

One of the greatest times in any woman's life is when she falls in love, becomes engaged, and is married. In that moment, she is close to God, goodness, and supreme happiness. When she thinks it can never get any better, she is then blessed with children and family.

And so it was that Lee and I decided to begin our own family. We waited eight years, however, before doing so as we felt there were too many goals and objectives to be met first. We knew that we could always go back to our respective businesses, but had only once chance with children. It was our passionate belief that nothing should ever interfere with the time we would spend with them.

I did not discuss my pregnancy with anyone but our immediate families. It was a special secret shared with only Lee, his mother Anna, and Helen. Instead, I camouflaged it to the best of my ability and was very discrete, continuing to model until I was five-and-a-half months along and then my tummy suddenly popped. Then I concentrated on growing my business, working throughout my ninth month.

One day, while fitting a wonderful Greek customer named Elena with false eyelashes, Helen mentioned that I was expecting my first child. That night after dinner, when Elena read her tea leaves, she received a vision and called me the next day to inform me that I would have a son.

"Darling!" I happily told Lee that night. "We're going to have a son!" He was, of course, as excited at the news as I was.

Elena was correct in that I would indeed have a son—but it would not be during this pregnancy.

The following week, a lovely client by the name of Rivian Hartman visited my salon for a new look in makeup and new eyelashes. It was difficult not to notice that her own tummy was even bigger than mine and we engaged in "baby conversation."

"When are you having yours?" I asked, cutting Rivian's lashes.

"February 1st," she said. "How about you?"

"February 14th," I answered proudly. "We hope to have a special Valentine's baby." As Rivian and I continued chatting, we discovered that her own doctor happened to be the partner of my obstetrician. At that time, neither Rivian nor I could have possibly imagined the series of coincidences that would continue to parallel our lives.

When your baby moves for the first time, it's a moment that no expectant mother or father, if he's fortunate enough to be

In my first shop, teaching a client to put on false eyelashes

with her, ever forgets. In that final month, mine seemed to increasingly favor the art of tap-dancing over ballet. She moved constantly.

As I leaned over the display counter to fit Rivian's false lashes, my baby kicked, protesting any different posture. Somehow, I still remember that particular kick.

Rivian smiled knowingly. "Wouldn't it be interesting if we saw each other in passing at Northwestern Memorial Hospital?"

86

she said. "We must see compare notes when our lives calm down a bit."

My life *never* seemed to calm down.

Two weeks before my due date, I was diagnosed with toxemia after my blood pressure shot up to 250 over 140. Although I felt absolutely fine, I was nevertheless admitted to Northwestern as a precaution. I could not understand why I had to be there in the obstetrics ward for two days, watching everyone else have their babies.

Through it all, Lee was there beside me. The first night of my stay, not satisfied with the quality of the hospital's menu, he brought me dinner. Several hours later, as I walked him to the elevator to say good night, I noticed a man standing at the window of the room separating the newborns from the hallway.

His face was pressed close to the glass as he admired his new son. I was charmed with the pride he exuded. Looking from him to the little baby he waved at, I marveled that this child was an absolute clone of his father.

"What a strong, handsome baby," I congratulated him. "What is his name?"

"Adam Lindsey Hartman," he beamed.

Suddenly I remembered Rivian.

"Oh, my! I met your wife last week!" I said. "I'm Marilyn Miglin. How is Rivian?"

As it turned out, she had delivered Adam by Cesarean section and was still recovering from the anesthetic. She had not yet seen her son. Before returning to my room, I asked her husband, Allen, to give Rivian my best and to congratulate her on having such a beautiful child.

The next day, I demanded to be sent home. I was not having any contractions. I felt fine, and I did not wish to be there any longer. There were too many other things to prepare for. The following month, I was scheduled to model the spring import collections, one of the most important seasons in the fashion world. I intended to have my baby and be working again one week later.

After two weeks, when it was really time for my baby to be born, I returned to the hospital. For hours, she moved around, but nothing else happened. Finally, the doctor tried to induce labor, but many hours later, the nurses informed me that I was not about to have my baby that night, since I had not even begun to dilate.

"Don't worry," they said. "Babies always get delivered, but usually on their own time schedule."

Lee kissed me good night and went home.

Later that evening, I had the worst stomach cramps I have ever had in my life. When I finally called for help, the resident on call that night diagnosed me as being nervous and a bit highstrung. He administered a shot of morphine, which I later discovered should *never* have been given to a pregnant woman.

The morphine did help to calm me but a half hour later, however, I experienced an amazing *new* feeling. It seemed as though my body was heaving back and forth. My cramps became so painfully violent, I thought I would not live to see the morning.

All I could think of was, "What is going to happen to me when I go into labor? If I cannot handle this, how will I live through the delivery?"

For what seemed like an eternity, I lay alone, enduring a body out of control with increasing spasms and contractions. Then to my amazement, I finally realized what was happening—I *was* in labor and having the baby by myself!

Frantically, I called to the nurses down the hall, who were playing cards. One of them strolled in at a leisurely pace, prepared to advise me that I was being overly hysterical. She took one look at me, however, and yelled, "Call the doctor! She's delivering!"

Clutching my tummy, I watched the nurses scramble in their own panic and thought to myself, "Now who's being high-strung?"

They rushed me into the delivery room, where my baby and I waited for what seemed to be an eternity before my doctor arrived.

At 4:44 a.m. on February 15, our first child was finally born. But when I first saw her, my heart stopped.

So small, so very tiny, weighing only four pounds, three ounces—her color was blue and she was having difficulty breathing, having been drugged by the morphine I had received hours earlier.

By the time Lee arrived, he was ashen from worry. "I thought you said we were going to have a little boy," he said, although it was obvious to anyone who saw him that he could not have been more overjoyed, but worried about his new daughter.

Lee and I named her Marlena—a combination of both our names, and, of course, for Marlene Dietrich, whose shapely legs, Helen had coveted for me.

Meanwhile, the day after Marlena was born, Rivian Hartman, who was about to be discharged, stopped by my room to share her congratulations. What had been a chance meeting became more than coincidence. Rivian and her husband became two of our dearest friends. To this day, I am affectionately known as their son Adam's Catholic godmother, since I saw him even before Rivian.

It was touch and go with Marlena for three weeks and we were not sure she would live. I prayed and promised God that if He would save her, I would try to pay Him back in some way for that gift.

For those long, agonizing weeks we watched helplessly over Marlena, who was kept in an isolette under constant medical supervision. We spent nearly every moment looking in on her, while praying.

In between visits, Lee engaged in a shopping expedition, purchasing for his daughter the most exquisite all-white pram. My grandmother, meanwhile, redirected her own worry by hand-sewing beautiful white coverlets and pillows trimmed with pink.

To our absolute joy and relief, Marlena finally grew strong enough for us to bring her home. Ever the fashion model mother, I dressed up for the event in a beautiful imported Italian pink sweater with marabou trim. Poor Marlena sneezed all the way home.

That same day, amid all the excitement, our miniature poodle Muffy somehow managed to break her leg while leaping from a chair. I wrapped both howling dog and crying baby in warm blankets and carried them through the Chicago winter to the vet, where Muffy was ensconced in a cast up to her shoulder.

There I was, carrying my infant daughter and my helpless dog—and I had more confidence in holding the dog than my own baby.

That first night, Marlena cried and cried. . .and we held her, cradled her, and walked with her into the early hours of the morning. Only perpetual motion put her to sleep and when we stopped, she awoke shortly thereafter.

I knew nothing about babies. Helen had always instructed me never to hold anyone else's for fear that I might drop the infant. That, of course, did little to instill in me any confidence with my own daughter.

Since he came from a large family, Lee had more trust in his own parenting skills, but he worried about me. One of his first actions as a new father was to call his sister Eleanor, who happened to be a nurse, asking her to spend some time with Marlena

The model mother

and me. It was my sister-in-law who finally taught me how to bathe Marlena, since I had been afraid to do so.

She was still very frail, so small that she fit into her father's massive hands. Lee never failed to walk with her for hours every night. Sometimes, we took turns. She continued to sleep for only short bursts of time and it was not until the day before her first birthday that she, Lee and I, experienced our first night of uninterrupted sleep.

Ever the model and former showgirl, I would not get out of bed after delivering Marlena without strapping and binding my tummy, even though my doctor had advised that no one did that anymore. My grandmother had instructed, however, that this would keep my stomach flat, and she proved to be correct.

I *did* do that fashion show a week later, and no one suspected I had just had a baby.

Wheeling a beautiful white carriage, Helen and I proudly walked Marlena each day down Oak Street and Michigan Avenue, the model mother and her newborn model daughter, swaddled in beautiful linens embroidered in pink, and carefully dressed in the most fashionable clothes.

We worried, however, when Marlena did not begin speaking at the appropriate age. All she said was "Mama" and " Dah Dah." We read to her constantly and she loved her books, her blue eyes widening with delight at each new story, no matter how many times we read it over and over. But still, she did not speak. Over the next year, she held her dainty little hand out and silently pointed, instead, to whatever she desired.

The following summer, when Marlena was two-and-a-half, we took a trip to Aspen. As were driving through the beautiful Rocky Mountains, she suddenly pointed excitedly and burst out, "Daddy, look at the mountains!" Lee turned to me and grinned, the proudest daddy in the world. From that moment on, she spoke both fluently and with eloquence.

While business was flourishing, having multiple stores proved to be an increasingly frustrating problem. One evening, a security guard at the Hawthorn Mall, where one shop was located, felt it his duty to call and inform me that my employee had closed the store at 9:15 p.m., when in fact the mall itself

On the runway oat Marshall Field's soon after Marlena was born

closed at 9:30. It seemed that this location was becoming a bit too strict for my tastes if my own employee could not make the decision to close early when there were no customers. I made the decision to close that store permanently.

Meanwhile, I discovered that the manager of another store was not paying the salon's bills. When she abruptly moved to another city without warning, I was forced to close that location as well.

After careful consideration and discussions with Lee, I decided that in order to balance work and quality time with Marlena, it was in our best interest to close all of the additional salons and concentrate fully on the Oak Street flagship store.

My beautiful daughter was becoming quite a handful and it was all I could do to manage both my personal and professional lives.

Several times while entertaining with dinner parties, I had enlisted the assistance of a wonderful cook named Gertrude. Helping me in the kitchen to prepare for our guests, she had a special way with Marlena, who by now, had grown even faster and more mischievous. Lee was a protective father, allowing no one but Helen, his mother Anna, and my grandmother to be left alone with her. He sensed a special bond with Gertrude and suggested that we consider hiring her to prepare a daily meal and stay with Marlena through her afternoon nap, while I returned to the salon. Gertrude would be with us for the next twenty-five years and became a special part of our family.

Our daughter, meanwhile, fancied herself quite the artist. She loved to draw and create with colorful paints, chalk, and whatever else she could get her little hands on. The canvas upon which she created her masterpieces was unimportant to her. To little Marlena, it was all about expressing her "artistic" vision at any given moment. One day, while Gertrude was busy baking cookies, Marlena ran to living room and translated one such "vision" through brightly colored crayon—all over the back of my beautiful upholstered chair. Poor Gertrude was beside herself.

Marlena kept us all on our toes.

One afternoon, an extraordinary Native American gentleman wandered into the store. After looking around briefly, he zeroed in on me with an intense stare. Having been up all night long with Marlena who had been fussing, I had not slept a wink and looked awful.

"You look tired," he said.

As I began to explain the previous evening's trials with my daughter, this man waved his hand dramatically.

"You don't have to be tired, you know. Just because you did not sleep last night is no reason for you to look and feel the way you do."

"I beg your pardon," I managed to say. "What do you mean?"

"Let me sit down with you. I'll explain it."

Against my better judgement, I invited him into my office to talk. His name was Mr. Silvernail. For whatever reason, his demeanor and the tone of his voice was soothing and hypnotic. If someone could explain to me the solution to not being tired, given the hectic pace of my life, I was certainly willing to invest a few moments of my time to listen.

"Look at that light," he said. I followed his gesture toward a small lamp on my desk. "Simply take the energy from that lamp. You're brain doesn't *know* that you're tired. You're *telling* it that you're tired."

I looked from the lamp to Mr. Silvernail. The corners of his mouth turned upward ever-so-slightly as he watched my obvious puzzlement turn to fascination over this extraordinary observation.

Marlena's third birthday party

"There is energy everywhere," he continued. "It's all around us. Be ever mindful of that energy and its sources. Reach out and take it. Recharge your body, mind, and soul."

Mr. Silvernail's sage advice was well taken. As a result, I learned to take energy from wherever I could get it. I learned to turn off the confusion, quiet my brain and weary body, and control my own energy, keeping it in its place.

Three years later, Lee and I decided that it was time for a new addition to our family. During my second pregnancy, I suffered terribly from morning sickness. I also gained thirty-five pounds instead of the seven I had added with Marlena.

For several years, we had longed for a house in the country and spent many weekend afternoons driving through northwest rural areas looking for property. Despite my noticeably pregnant condition, I was scheduled to give a speech in Marengo,

Illinois, one afternoon. Lee felt that the distance was too far for me to drive alone and so he arranged to take the day off, personally chauffeuring me to my engagement. He provided curb-side delivery and while I was speaking, he managed to slip away into neighboring Woodstock to ascertain whether there were any houses for rent.

Upon picking me up after my speech, he drove to Woodstock, where we toured a house which we immediately decided to rent for the summer. Lee arranged a deposit and the three of us spent an absolutely enchanting summer there, with Helen joining us each weekend. Just before Labor Day, we received a wonderful surprise. Helen Maxwell, an heiress to a wallpaper fortune, had heard how much we adored her section of property and called Lee to determine our interest in purchasing a few acres of it.

We jumped at the chance and upon rushing over to view it, I was amazed to find nothing but pure, virgin forest. We made her an offer and were fortunate enough to purchase twenty-four acres. Lee walked and I "waddled" the property and together we made plans for a small house on a hill overlooking a valley filled with fields, woods, fens, and wetlands. Life there was simple and we looked forward to future family getaways where we would spend many happy days together.

Meanwhile, I did not think that I could get any larger. Just before entering the hospital, I cherished an afternoon I spent with Marlena, when she came home from nursery school.

"This is our special time together as a mommy and her little girl," I explained. "Tomorrow, we're going to have a new addition to our family."

I was sensitive to the fact that often, when one's second child is born, every bit of attention is focused upon the new baby. Lee and I took extra care to ensure that this would not happen and that Marlena would remain the center of attention.

When I went into labor this time, I allowed no one but my own doctor to touch me and refused any medication.

Our second baby, a healthy, seven-pound, eleven-ounce strapping boy, was born in four hours. We named him Duke, after John Wayne. The following morning, Lee brought Helen and Marlena to the hospital to escort us home.

On his first day home, as little boys do, he christened his white buggy and most of the dining room as I was diapering him, and I quickly learned the difference between changing a baby girl and a baby boy.

Unlike his sister, Duke began talking at a precociously early age. Sitting straight in his highchair, he commanded the attention of all the ladies in the Miglin household, who catered to his every wish and demand. He became known as the "Little King."

Father Fu, our family, and godparents Dorsey and John Forbes at Duke's baptism

He had a mind of his own and the most stubborn resolve of any child I have ever seen. Never could he be cajoled into drinking any more milk or eating what he did not want. Not Duke. When he was finished, that was it.

Lee continued to be an integral part of my support system. Together, we stuffed envelopes announcing sales and promotions until two and three in the morning. When Duke began to fuss in Helen's apartment on the third floor above us, I would merely retrieve him for a midnight feeding and then continue to lick stamps until we had finished. Lee would hop into his car with several enormous bags of mail and race off to the post office shouting, "Be right back!"

When Duke turned two-and-a-half, Lee and I grew more excited about his forthcoming enrollment in the same Head Start program that Marlena had enjoyed. I was livid upon discovering that the program's funding had been cut. Marching into the principal's office, I expressed my rage and asked what I could do. I was not about to go away quietly, accepting the fact that some bureaucrat in Washington had decided that the opportunities afforded by programs such as Head Start were unimportant in shaping the lives of the nation's children.

It must be said that there is little that can stand in the way of a mob of angry mothers and I took it upon myself to organize such a group. We traveled to Washington to plead our case, and there I addressed a Senate subcommittee demanding the reinstatement of funding. I was never so nervous in my life, but I was not about to leave without securing that money.

In the end, the funding for Head Start was indeed renewed. Although the hours were shortened, Duke and many other children went on to enjoy the same opportunity his sister had.

One morning, when I picked Duke up from school, he was wearing only one shoe.

Duke, two years old

"What happened to his other shoe?" I asked a teacher.

"I have no idea."

"But how could he lose just one?"

"Well," she said, "we're not sure."

"What did you do with your shoe?" I asked Duke when we got into the car. He looked ahead and said nothing.

"What could you have possibly done with it," I demanded. "Did you put it down the toilet? Tell me what you did with that shoe!"

He merely shrugged. Obviously he had no intention of sharing with me its whereabouts.

This mystery reminded me of a similar incident when Marlena also suddenly lost a shoe on our way to one of my fittings at Marshall Field's. In her little white buggy, one of her designer shoes had simply vanished. I never found it and I never did learn what had happened to Duke's shoe.

I decided, instead, that my children apparently had a strong aversion to footwear and later bronzed each of their remaining shoes. Today, rather than two complete pairs, I have only one bronzed shoe for each of them.

In the coming years, our children would give us much to be proud of.

Meanwhile, as a young working mother, I encountered the same problems that so many mothers face—I wanted to be with my children as much as possible and still be successful in my business. It did not take me long to realize that my first priority would always be my family. It was more than the "quality time" that so many women's books and magazines promote. I knew that work would always be there, but that all too soon my children would grow up and leave to make their own lives in the world.

I was determined that I could be a full-time mother *and* a successful entrepreneur. You have but one chance to raise your children and you must always give one-hundred-ten percent. Because I believed so strongly in family, I brought this philosophy into my business and encouraged my employees to think the same way. If a woman working for me had a sick child or needed to attend a school program, she could take a day or an afternoon off without fear of job reprisal that even today is so common in the workplace. The unexpected benefit from this policy has been a loyalty from my employees that few other business owners enjoy.

My favorite model for my products

I ran my business, I took care of my babies, and I managed my home, and my real estate.

The secret to doing this all successfully was being organized. Marlena and Duke still laugh about it, but I had my meals planned in advance for each week. Mondays were known as "soup night," and of course, on Fridays, following Catholic tradition, I always prepared fish.

The rest of the week was divided up into basic foods like chops, chicken, steak, and ham. Each morning I set the table before leaving for work, so that when I came home in the evening, all I had to do was turn on the oven and then change into more comfortable clothes while dinner was cooking.

Every day, I was the first to arise, hair blown dry and makeup applied before coming downstairs to make breakfast for my family. Lee always squeezed fresh orange juice and became a connoisseur in brewing marvelous coffee, although he rarely drank it. Each morning, we sat down together as a family, discussing our respective plans for the day that lay ahead. I packed the children's lunches and together, my husband and I drove or walked them to school.

Although most of the other parents in our neighborhood sent their children to private schools, Lee and I felt that it was important for Marlena and Duke to be exposed to more diversity and they attended the Ogden Elementary Public School, halfway between our home and my salon. Since I had received a good education in the Chicago system, I was sure my daughter and son would as well.

I became active at Ogden as a volunteer and involved myself in my children's extra-curricular activities. They both participated in sports. Marlena took dance and piano lessons, and when Duke was old enough to join the Cub Scouts, I became a den mother. The meetings were held at our house and sometimes we held special activities.

One such project was a swimming event at a nearby YMCA, so the boys could obtain their swimming badges. One little boy named Robert hesitated, and so I instructed him to jump into the water. He did so, but immediately began floundering, sputtering, and then went under. To my horror, it quickly became apparent that Robert was drowning. Duke and his friend, Mark Lemkuhl, pulled him out.

"Why on earth did you jump into that pool when you don't know how to swim?" I asked after ascertaining that he was unharmed.

"Well," he stammered, "because you told me to."

"Then you have now learned one of the most important lessons in life," I gently advised him, "and that is to know how to admit that you don't know something."

Later, at a special Scout meeting, Duke and Mark, who had saved Robert's life, were awarded a special medal of merit.

When Marlena was about ten years old, her friends became intrigued by modeling, so I ran a "Miss Manners" class for them at home. I taught them how to sit and walk like a model, the proper use of utensils, and when to say please and thank you. My belief in the importance of feeling good about yourself was reinforced by their happy faces as they carefully walked around our living room with books on their heads to help their posture. No matter what your age, self-confidence comes from self-knowledge.

At the end of each school day, Marlena and Duke often came to the salon, where they did their homework in the quiet of Helen's apartment upstairs, or in my office. Then they helped out around the store, cleaning and doing small chores. Helen would sometimes drive them to their after-school activities and spent wonderful quality time with them.

I returned home every evening by six p.m. to cook dinner, and no matter how busy he was, Lee made sure he was there in

Teaching modeling at Marshall Field's

time for dinner, too. Once the children were in bed, he would return to the office, working late into the night.

Our house became the stable center of their lives, a place where their classmates were always welcome and where we celebrated birthday parties and holiday festivities with family and friends. It gave me an inner strength because we had a family goal. It was, and still is, a focus for my energy—a support, a refuge, and my protection.

Weekends were always reserved for family activities. We never accepted any social engagements on Sunday. That was our special time together. We also spent a great deal of time at our country getaway in Woodstock.

From the beginning, Marlena loved animals—*all* animals. It seemed at times that our home resembled a veterinary clinic. When she found an injured pigeon we brought it home, nursing it back to good health. In the country, she discovered a baby field mouse, which also shared our home until he became strong enough to be returned to the wild.

With a steady stream of injured squirrels, turtles, our black poodle Muffy, and a cat named Mary, we had a full house with no vacancies. I suppose that I did not exactly help to alleviate the "Miglin Home for Wayward Creatures." One evening at a charity event that Lee and I attended, I was horrified to find a canary being used as a silent auction item. Like Marlena, I have a soft spot in my heart for all living things and could not bear to see this poor bird suffering, not knowing where he would wind up.

Naturally, Lee placed a bid on the bird. We were taken aback when the bidding reached five hundred dollars. We purchased the bird for that amount, Lee sighed good-naturedly, and "Dickie" the canary became part of our family, living with us for many years.

One day while visiting a neighboring farm in Woodstock to gather fresh eggs, the farmer's wife happened to mention to Marlena and Duke that her dog recently had puppies. "Would you like one?" she asked.

What do children say when someone asks, "Would you like a puppy?" So, we acquired yet another family member that afternoon and named her Ginger.

Meanwhile, George Fiedler, my New York cosmetic chemist, lost his company, and offered to work for me.

The Miglin family, with some of our pets

In the lab with Dr. Fiedler and my family

His misfortune became my blessing, and when the tenant on the second floor above my salon moved out, I established a laboratory there, where Dr. Fiedler could do all of our research and development. He moved into the apartment building we owned across the street from our house. His wife Sylvia remained in New York, where he would visit as often as he could.

Always wearing a lab coat, he frequently came down into the shop to show me the new products he was developing. Each time he did so, I introduced him to everyone in the salon; people were very impressed that I had a chemist working for me.

We were photographed by newspapers and magazines working together on new "creations," which made marvelous press for the salon. Dr. Fiedler *loved* it!

When I wanted a new product, his usual response would be, "It can't be done, Marilyn! It can't be done!" But I would push and cajole him. "George, try it anyway." And he would, because he loved the challenge. He was a walking encyclopedia of information and took great pride and personal pleasure in sharing his knowledge.

Since Dr. Fiedler was alone in Chicago, he frequently joined us for dinner. He became our children's confidant and a beloved Jewish grandfather figure, who would often play chess with Marlena. Our conversations at the table were always about new products, what makes a good formulation, about skin care, and some religion. These were my children's dinner conversations— it taught both Marlena and Duke invaluable lessons in work ethics.

I happen to believe that confidence is an attribute we are born with, but often lose during our awkward teen years. If we believe in ourselves and our dreams, we regain confidence later in life. Certainly, it is the main ingredient of success.

Knowledge is power and that is what I try to pass on to other women—the power to bring out the best in themselves, the beauty that is already there.

It seemed that my dreams had become a reality and despite the difficulties of maintaining the day-to-day activities of home and business, I could not have asked for more, nor have been more content.

How could I have known what fate had in store, or of forthcoming adventures that would take me to the far corners of the world.

CHAPTER FOUR

"How do you make your dreams come true? You do it by being just as enthusiastic about the success of others as you are about your own success."

Sometimes, success comes from listening to others. You can discover a power to both guide and alter the course of your life.

For me, that voice came from my own clients. They kept saying, "When are you going to create a perfume that will make me smell as beautiful as I look when I wear your makeup?"

"Why shouldn't I?" I thought. All of the fashion designers were creating their own scents.

I happen to think that wearing fragrance is the finishing touch; it's our invisible fashion accessory and puts air in one's tires. How nice it would be, I thought, to have my own special perfume, something for the woman of today.

In my naiveté, I had not stopped to consider exactly how I would go about creating such a fragrance, but I believe in destiny.

Never do I close the door to new ideas or potential opportunities. I happen to be a girl who cannot say no, and if my clients wished for me to develop a perfume, then I was determined to make the best one in the world for them.

Never did I realize, of course, just how challenging this might be. Because New York is the center of the fragrance industry, that is where I began. In Chicago, at that time, all we had were industrial chemists. I needed to find someone with a "nose" to work with—a person who formulated perfumes.

And so, I excitedly scheduled my appointments with the top fragrance houses in New York City. During my meetings with these gentlemen (and of course, they were *all* men), I explained to them that I wished to create a scent unlike any other, a perfume that would empower the modern woman, so different that it would be heralded as an all-time classic.

They gave me five bottles of perfume and asked which one I liked, explaining they would be more than happy to manufacture it for me. The samples they set before me, however, smelled very much like those *already* being sold.

They explained that the industry followed certain trends and that the fragrances were the latest.

"No, no," I protested. "You must ask me about the woman of today! We need to explore why she wears perfume and what it is she wants from it. Please understand that I want to work *with* you to create a scent that captures an inner spirit—one that will enhance a woman's intelligence and independence.

These days," I explained, "women are using it for their own pleasure, not to please men, because it makes them feel good."

"We work in ten year cycles," was the answer. "These are the scents that are currently in vogue."

I simply could not believe what I was hearing.

"But I wish to work *with* you to create something that has never been done before," I said.

"We are the experts. This is the way the industry works, and if you wish to have a perfume, you will have to abide by our standards. What you want is simply not done."

I was incredulous that these men refused to explore new possibilities and assist me in developing a new fragrance through what I knew in my heart to be the correct approach. None of them were willing to work with me to formulate a unique perfume.

So Lee and I traveled to France, the birthplace of modern fragrance. I was sure that the French perfumers would be much more receptive to my vision and better understand what it was that I sought to create.

In Paris and the perfume houses of Grasse, using my best French, I carefully articulated my desire to create for American women a perfume unlike anything developed before.

Needless to say, I was quite surprised when the chemists offered me a choice of seven bottles. They suggested that I choose whichever one I liked best and they would manufacture it for me. My treatment was identical to that which I had received in New York, and I could hardly believe the insensitivity of these experts.

Again, when I explained that I wished to be directly involved in the creation of the perfume that would bear my name, I was informed that this would not be possible.

"We are the experts, Madame."

Frustrated and defeated, we returned to Chicago and by then I knew I had to learn more about fragrance, its history, how it is made, and about the industry itself. I needed to develop an expertise in order to be taken seriously.

I began my quest only blocks from my salon at Chicago's Newberry Library, one of the most respected research libraries in the country. I looked up the word "perfume" and that began several years of intensive research, feverishly devouring every book I could find which detailed any information on perfume and its origins.

For three-and-a-half years, my bedside reading revolved around fragrance, and through sheer determination I became quite well-versed in the subject. Throughout all of my research, however, two pieces of information stayed with me.

One was the scientific documentation of pheromones, a word first coined in 1959 by American scientists. These are natural chemicals or scents which trigger a specific response. They are found in most living things. "Pheromone" translated literally, means an organic substance used to communicate. How interesting, I thought, that pheromones were a nonverbal, nonvisual means of communication, not unlike perfume.

Every university in the country was doing research on isolating human pheromones. They had indeed been able to isolate them in insects and animals, but found that the human female had ten-thousand individual scent signals. As of yet, the scientific community does not know which one attracts a member of the opposite sex.

Even more fascinating to me, were the romantic origins of fragrance in ancient Egypt, where certain scents were considered more precious than gold. It was there, in the land of the Pharaohs, that perfume began.

The Egyptians believed that perfume created a positive magic aura around a person, promoting good health and stimulating spiritual awareness. They understood that it evoked a behavioral response. They revered unguents and oils for their powers and used them to influence others.

Ancient high priests burned droplets of special tree resins, releasing scented fumes that filled the temples, setting them apart from all other places. Kings of Egypt also desired to possess the mystical effects these heady scents provided.

In ancient times, for a scent to achieve notoriety, the finished product had to have an aura of rarity, exclusiveness, and of the Divine—the more exotic the ingredients, the more valued the commodity.

The Pharaoh's viziers and ministers brought caravans from all over the world, laden with precious herbs and spices and the seeds of exotic plants, which produced scented sweet and pungent oils. Traders from lands far away came with lines of camels bearing scented treasures for royalty: cinnamon, myrrh, lotus, oil of palm, juniper, nutmeg, almond oil, saffron, camphor, and golden honey.

These treasures were bestowed upon the Pharaoh's chemists, who experimented with pressing, heating, cooking, mixing and matching them until wonderful and pleasing aromas emerged. The recipe for each fragrance was then duly recorded and presented to the Pharaoh, becoming his personal property—his royal signature scent.

It was absolutely spellbinding to me that these people in a golden land so long ago, possessed such knowledge about fragrance.

That modern science was just beginning to back up with facts what this ancient civilization had taken on faith, that scent is a powerful thing, was amazing to me. The Egyptians had instinctively understood this and while the science of scent was relatively new in 1976, those people were already quite knowledgeable on the subject long ago. They actually possessed the ability to unlock that power.

I became utterly engrossed with this glorious culture and simply had to learn more. There was no better place to do so than the University of Chicago's Oriental Institute, where I began to attend lectures and enrolled in classes. There, I spoke with Egyptologists, pulling from them every minute detail I could on the subject of fragrance.

I think that I probably amused many of the professors with my endless questions and curiosity. In fact, I became quite notorious among the staff, who came to respect my passion.

In 1976, President Nixon reopened trade with Egypt and the University of Illinois' Department of Egyptology excitedly arranged an archeological expedition, gaining approval from the Egyptian government to visit ancient tombs and temples normally closed to tourists and Western scholars. Because of my great enthusiasm in learning everything possible about ancient Egypt, I happened to know each of the members in this group.

My mantra happens to be that success is when opportunity meets preparation. At the last possible moment—just two days before the group was scheduled to depart for Egypt—two of the professors were afforded their own opportunity to accept fellowships at the University. Both accepted, leaving two vacancies in the expedition.

In one of those moments, which so gloriously defines serendipity, several faculty members suggested that Lee and I take the place of those who were unable to go.

Needless to say, he was as thrilled as I was at the invitation and this marvelous opportunity. We hurriedly made the necessary arrangements for Marlena and Duke, packed our bags, and prepared to accept this most unexpected gift that life had offered.

There is a reason for everything. Certainly, it was not my expectation in traveling to Egypt to find a perfume. I went out of curiosity. I expected only to have a wonderful adventure and I have not been the same since.

Late one January day in 1977, tired after a long flight to Cairo, I found myself shielding my eyes from the intense sunshine reflected off the airport tarmac. This was certainly a change from the bleak winter landscape we had left behind in Chicago.

During those first few moments in Cairo's old airport, amid the hustle and bleating car horns, I was suddenly swept away to another place in time. I turned and looked west toward a setting desert sun, silhouetting the three Great Pyramids of Giza dramatically poised upon the horizon just across the Nile.

I remember little else of our exhausted arrival, not passing through customs, nor the drive through crowded streets to the Nile Hilton Hotel. My mind was clouded with visions of ancient times in the land of the Pharaohs. To see the majestic monuments, relive lives past, and travel ancient byways was to be one of the greatest experiences in my life.

Our first morning in Egypt was spent aboard a large, chartered bus, which took us one-hundred-seventy miles inland to the city of Beni Hassan. There we visited ancient tombs nestled high in the cliffs above the Nile River.

When we returned to the motor coach, a curious thing happened. An old man, with dark skin wrinkled and leather-like from years in the harsh desert sun, caught my attention and smiled at me. When I returned his smile, he silently pushed into my hand a small feather. His actions were deliberate, as though returning something I had dropped.

When I took my seat on the bus, I looked around to see if any of the others had received the same gift. But no one else carried a feather.

I turned to look for the old man, but he had disappeared. As the bus pulled away, I opened a book and began to read. Occasionally, I lifted my head to gaze at the landscape passing by, slipping the feather between the pages of my book to mark my place.

Our bus headed south along the east bank of the Nile. The city of Cairo gave way to long stretches of sandy desert. It was only along the banks of the Nile that we could see greenery.

My two-week journey was an arduous one as it was not a tourist jaunt, but rather an archeological expedition. I crawled on my stomach through narrow passageways and caves alongside scholars and Egyptologists, searching for information and artifacts.

Our tour began hundreds of miles up the Nile at Luxor, near the Valley of the Kings. Over the course of the next eleven days, we worked our way back down the Nile River. We climbed steep and craggy cliffs to examine tombs and spectacular temples adorned with hieroglyphics and elaborate carvings.

I shall never forget the sights—such as the juxtaposition of a small donkey, with a tattered leather harness, grazing between a modern pickup truck and a gleaming Mercedes Benz—the ancient and new worlds coexisting peacefully, side-by-side. The Egyptians have a word for this: *Maat.* "As it was . . . as it is . . . as it always will be."

The trip did have some similarities to the movie, *Raiders of the Lost Ark*, especially when I got lost in the desert.

Everyone in our group mounted a camel in order to reach the entrance of the Valley of the Kings. I had ridden horses when I was a young girl, but riding a camel was certainly much different than being seated on a docile horse while trotting along the equestrian path in Lincoln Park bordering Lake Michigan.

When my camel decided that he had grown tired of our slow pace, he took off at a gallop. Hanging on to the saddle, my only concern was with not falling off and being trampled. When at last he finally stopped, I suddenly realized we were alone, surrounded by barren desert, with no one and nothing else in sight.

Fortunately, Lee found me. Needless to say I was both overjoyed and terribly relieved to see him.

On the fifth day, we boarded the *Nile Steamer*, a rustic old ship that would become our floating hotel for the next week. Actually, it could better be described as a *rusted* old steamship, which appeared to be an errant set-piece from an old Humphrey Bogart movie.

Stepping out of the cabin, I expected to see characters like Peter Lorre or Sydney Greenstreet lingering at the rail, or a dark, mysterious man wearing a Turkish fez, nervously pacing the deck.

After a few days moored in Luxor, our floating hotel began winding its way down the Nile toward Giza and the Great Pyramids. We awakened to spectacular sunrises and the days were filled with sensory delights that ranged from the scent of jasmine and lotus flowers to the visual beauty of reeds, rushes and papyrus growing along the banks of the river. The nights were ushered in by lavish sunsets painting the sky brilliant hues of orange, red and purple, quickly fading into the proverbial night of a thousand stars.

I was traveling along the same waterway as Cleopatra, who drenched her legendary barge with perfumes and fragrant oils to enchant and seduce Mark Anthony. Historians say she likely wore many scents on different parts of her body. Perhaps the essence of cardamom and cinnamon in her hair, iris root, saffron, and myrrh on her body, and lotus and almond oils on the soles of her feet. Her throne stood enveloped in a cloud of pungent sweetness curling upward from incense burners below.

Many years later Shakespeare would write of Anthony and Cleopatra, "Purple the sails and so perfumed that the winds were lovesick." Slaves and royalty alike stood on the river's banks drinking in the sweet fragrance of Cleopatra's barge wafting through the night as it drifted down the same route I now found myself traveling.

When we arrived in Cairo, we were granted special permission from the Egyptian government to enter the Pyramid of

Menkaure—a privilege accorded only to historians and archeological experts.

Buried in the tomb were gold, perfumes, and perfume recipes to aid the spirits of the deceased. I was told that grave robbers stole the perfumed oils first. Then, if they still had time, inclination, and room in their pockets, they grabbed the gold. Looters thoroughly destroyed the interiors of this great structure over the centuries.

Standing at the base of this massive stone monument, I was overcome with awe. To see any one of the pyramids up close is overwhelming. It took decades to complete each one, and even today, no one knows how such massive limestone blocks were moved and fitted perfectly into place.

There were no steps or ramps, so we scaled piles of rubble, balancing our way across narrow wooden planks, and then crawling into a hot, dusty, dark passageway. Far back in this tunnel, several young Egyptian boys positioned themselves at each major turning point.

Two of them had scrambled ahead before any of our archeological study group entered, while one remained at the small opening leading to the pharaoh's chamber, nearly one-hundred feet up from the base of the pyramid.

This boy held in his hands a mirror, nearly two feet square, that reflected a brilliant beam of desert sunlight into the small dark opening. Perhaps thirty yards into the tunnel, the next one positioned himself with another mirror, reflecting the beam around a corner toward a second opening.

As we crawled through the hot and dusty passageways, I peered through the dimly lit corridor straining to see the light. The entrance grew so narrow that I was barely able to pull myself past the second boy, who did not speak, but nodded reassuringly.

Because of the narrow passageways, a government official accompanying us asked that we enter the Pharaoh's chamber one at a time. I went first.

The initial descent was easy. It consisted of a square opening approximately five feet high, angled slightly downward for about thirty yards. Because I could not walk upright, navigating the corridor became an interesting trick as I crouched over in the darkness, feeling my way along the walls.

When I reached the end of the passageway, I returned the smile of another boy awaiting me. His grin was as bright as the beam of light being reflected around the corner to light my way.

Not knowing what lay just beyond, I turned the corner with great trepidation. However, rather than more cramped tunnels, I emerged into an enormous, open hallway with a level floor, perhaps sixty feet long and fifteen feet wide, with walls at least twenty feet high. No one had prepared me for this, and I marveled at having discovered this spectacular gallery.

Beams of sunlight reflecting off surfaces of polished floor-to-ceiling granite created deep shadows in the carved hieroglyphs, telling stories of ancient people and events. Removing one glove, I traced my fingers lightly over the carvings. While I could not read their message, I certainly felt their energy.

At the end of this gallery stood the third boy. He too smiled, nodded and gestured to my left, where his mirror bounced a beam of sunlight into a small hole no more than three feet square. Taking a deep breath, I put on my glove and climbed the small pile of rubble below the opening. No more than ten feet into the space, I knew that this would be difficult to navigate.

Since my body filled nearly the entire passageway, there was little light to show the way. I often found myself moving ahead blindly. Suddenly, the stone floor beneath me became rough hewn wood and I knew that I had arrived—somewhere.

As I inched through the small opening, a shaft of sunlight softly illuminated a larger room in front of me. The richness of the beautiful carvings indicated to me that I had finally reached the pharaoh's royal chamber. I had entered Menkaure's secret burial place.

I crawled out of small hole in the wall, nearly four feet above the floor and onto a crude, wooden platform resembling a table. Swinging my legs around and over the edge, I gently dropped to the floor. I brushed my gloved hands together and rubbing my knees, I launched a five-thousand year old cloud of dust that I wished I had not.

Reaching into my pocket for the small flashlight that each member of our expedition carried, I scanned every wall with great care. There, above the empty sarcophagus where the Pharaoh once rested, I saw a deeply carved cartouche of Menkaure, King of Egypt and the fifth ruler of the Fourth Dynasty in the Old Kingdom.

To the right of the sarcophagus stood a stone platform resembling a banquet table. Having viewed previous tombs during our trip, I knew that was where the pharaoh's most treasured belongings had been enshrined to accompany him on his long journey to eternity.

I noticed a dusty broken urn lying at the base of the stone table. Others lay scattered nearby. Kneeling to pick one up, I was amazed to catch a faint scent unlike any I had ever before encountered. As I brought it closer, the distinctive fragrance became stronger and more pervasive.

How could it have lasted upon that earthen vase for almost five thousand years?

I stooped to examine another shard only to discover another scent. And another, and still another, each with its own distinctive odor. Some sweet, some bitter, some quite pungent, but still there after thousands of years. My first instinct was to keep one, but remembering what I had been told by the government offi-

Within a tomb filled with hieroglyphics

cial forbidding the removal of even the tiniest pebble from the sacred shrines, I carefully replaced each one, precisely as I had found it.

Suddenly the thought struck me that if the odor of those perfumes could still persist, there had to be a way to duplicate those formulas for use in a modern perfume.

Spreading out some paper I had brought along, I made rubbings of the hieroglyphic perfume recipes etched upon the tomb walls and folded them into my pocket.

I knew that I must leave so that others could enjoy the same richness and turned for one last look. I strained to envision someone standing at the wall, carving these messages for his pharaoh and for eternity. In my mind, I thanked him—and with each scent forever locked in my mind, I vowed to learn what it was he was trying to tell me.

When the members of our group finally rejoined each other, I excitedly detailed my discovery. An Egyptologist, Farag El

Gabry, offered to translate some of the perfume recipes I had traced from the stone walls of the chamber. I was astonished to learn that some of the perfumed oils were comprised of over forty ingredients, including cyprinium and mendesium and other complex compounds.

Then fate stepped in again.

Farag offered to introduce me to his father, who happened to be a perfumer in Cairo. It was as though God had sent me to Egypt to learn what I needed to know to produce a very special perfume.

We returned to Cairo for dinner that evening and I met Farag's father. When he finally understood that I wished to duplicate the ingredients in the formula I had found, he was horrified.

"These are old. They *smell* old," he said, "Like an old church. We do not use these anymore. I make for you a copy of a French perfume, instead."

"No, please," I begged. "Please, I will pay you to reproduce the ingredients in the hieroglyphics."

Reluctantly, he did so, and I could not wait to try what he gave me. Unfortunately, he was absolutely right. The smells were awful and all I can say is that they indeed belonged to a different era.

What's more, the odor they left on my skin where I had tried them remained curiously strong and persisted, even after repeated washing. Three days later, I could still smell them.

How different from the perfumes that I had been using at home which lasted all of ten minutes. There was something unique to these formulations, and I had to find out what it was.

I was eager now to return to Chicago in order to undertake the challenge of understanding the properties of these oils. As I packed, I rediscovered the old man's feather, still marking a page on the ancient art of Egyptian perfumery in one of my books.

Outside a pyramid entrance

Nearly moved to tears, I was overcome by an indescribable feeling of fate.

After four years of research and travel, I was bringing home a recipe that would become the catalyst for a fragrance to empower every woman who wore it.

We returned to Chicago with great excitement and anticipation. Immediately, I began searching for someone who could assist me in unraveling answers to these puzzling formulations. Finally, after a year, I heard of a young Italian perfumer in New York named Vito Lenoci.

When I met with Vito, I asked if he had ever worked with any of the ingredients I had discovered.

"No, I have not," he said.

"Could you eliminate some of the cloying notes for me?" I inquired.

"I would like to work with you," he hesitated, "but how do I know that you can 'smell'?"

I knew I had a good nose for smells. My aunt used to take me shopping and we would open bottles and other foods to smell them to determine whether or not they were fresh.

Vito suggested that I take a smell test.

"Fine," I agreed.

Blindfolded, I was asked to identify basic odors such as citrus, lavender, and basil. Then these essences were mixed together, and I was asked to identify each part of the compound. I successfully passed the test, and this is how Pheromone began.

For the next year-and-a-half, Vito and I worked to refine, enhance, and modernize my formulation. Using a multitude of "absolutes"—derivatives from wild grasses to exotic barks, from Ylang-Ylang to lotus and palm oils—each ingredient was processed separately, then combined. The resulting fragrance proved to be the ultimate example of the Egyptian art form developed after centuries of experimentation.

Of all the ingredients, jasmine was and still is the costliest. More than one million blossoms are needed to make one pound of essential oil. The process is both expensive and time-consuming, as jasmine flowers bloom only at night and must be picked before daybreak.

We used tonka extract from a rare tree, which grows only in Venezuela, where the seeds are dried in the sun before being soaked in rum. The delicate tree that bears the orange blossoms used in my recipe takes twelve years to mature before it bears its first bloom. One tree produces only six pounds of flowers and it takes approximately ten-thousand pounds to make one pound of essential oil.

I am a lady who never settles for anything less than the highest of quality. I insisted upon using the "enfleurage" method of extracting the oil from the flowers. It is the most expensive and time-consuming method of doing so, but also the finest. Using this process, petals are pressed into wax. The petals are changed daily, until the wax is saturated with oil. This method thereby protects delicate floral unguents that could otherwise be affected by heat.

Certain essences were extracted by distillation—the flowers picked at just the right moment and placed into vats before being steamed to separate the oil from the flowers. Maintaining the correct temperature is essential, for if the steam is too hot it can alter the oils, if too cool, the batch is completely ruined.

After seven years of research and development, my masterpiece fragrance, drawn from the sands of time, was finally in hand. What emerged was an evocative bouquet of one-hundred seventy-nine rare and costly essences, including wine resins and oils imported from France, Italy, Belgium, Madagascar, Portugal, and of course, Egypt.

I decided to name it *Pheromone.* Literally, the word means to communicate and that, of course, is what I believe fragrance is all about—a form of silent communication.

 It did not take long for me to discover that my new fragrance did indeed both stimulate and communicate. The very first day I wore it when leaving the New York laboratories, people in elevators smiled. Even my gruff and tough cab driver looked into the rearview mirror and asked, "Hey, lady! What are you wearing? Smells good!" All day long, men took notice and women inquired.

All was not smooth sailing, however.

First, the Madison Avenue advertising and marketing types argued that Pheromone was not a good name. Nobody would be able to pronounce it, they said. No one could remember the name and nobody would understand its meaning.

I held my ground.

The second major obstacle came in holding fast to my passion for the natural ingredients used in Pheromone. Again, the marketing people said, "You can't do that. It's much too expensive. You must use synthetics to reduce the cost."

Reluctantly, I agreed to allow the chemists to make it in a synthetic form. I tried that for only one or two days, but the quality was just not there. "I cannot do this," I rationalized. "This is *my* name—*my* creation!"

I knew that people would be willing to spend money to experience quality. I also happen to believe that one forgets about price long after continuing to enjoy the quality of that product. Of course, any woman would be willing to invest in something that would keep her feeling beautiful and sensual all day long and late into the evening, until stepping into her bath or shower.

My exacting blend of ingredients would remain all and *only* natural. For its packaging, I chose an elegant crystal bottle shaped like an obelisk, the Egyptian phallic symbol for strength and harmony. I then sent the finished product in unmarked

127

bottles to some of my customers around the country and asked them to comment honestly about the fragrance. As I had anticipated, the response was overwhelmingly positive.

My decisions were difficult. I followed my heart and in doing so, I went against what every other perfumer was doing at the time; I decided to make the most expensive perfume on the market. But I believed in what I was doing.

Despite the marketing people's "professional" advice, the introductory price of three-hundred dollars the ounce generated an instant mystique and priceless publicity (today, Pheromone retails for five-hundred dollars an ounce).

I used a marketing technique that included sending messages and phone calls to buyers at upscale department stores. My personal approach, determination, and follow-through finally allowed me to secure appointments to see them.

Angelo Manolis, the divisional merchandise manager at Marshall Field & Company gave me my first chance at the flagship store on State Street in Chicago—with one stipulation. I had one month to sell-through my order. If sales for Pheromone were in any way lax, that would be the end.

I received my first order, shipped it, did some promotions, and then I prayed.

Then, a curious thing happened. One morning, Wally Phillips, a legend on Chicago radio, received a call from a woman who shared with his listeners a frustrating experience. It seemed that her husband had been following another woman around at a party the previous Saturday evening, exclaiming aloud to all within earshot his passion for the perfume she was wearing, something called "Phroom." This frustrated wife was desperate to get her hands on this perfume for herself, but did not know where to purchase it.

"Phroom?" said Wally. "What kind of a name is that?"

Shortly after that another listener called and suggested that it might be Pheromone, adding that her daughter was studying about pheromones in biology class.

Wally then called Marshall Field's where a sales associate confirmed that the fragrance in question was indeed Pheromone from Marilyn Miglin, a fact which he shared with his listeners. Further, he called my office the following day and put me on-air to discuss this new fragrance that had apparently driven his listener's husband wild.

Opportunity meets preparation? And was I ever prepared to discuss my beautiful perfume!

"You know ladies and gentlemen," I said, "the word *phero-mone* means an organic substance used to communicate—and gentlemen, that is precisely what I had in mind when I created it."

Later that day, Marshall Field's was inundated with taxi drivers who had been listening to the radio. They streamed into the State Street store, snatching up bottles of Pheromone and I sold out in less than two days.

I personally secured appointments with each fragrance buyer, and the passion I exuded for my beautiful perfume proved contagious. Over the next three years, I successfully gained a foothold in both the Texas and California markets. Before long, Pheromone was being distributed in nearly every state west of the Mississippi. I was determined to build upon the momentum I had gained.

Marketing proved to be challenging. Because I was still relatively unknown, many department store buyers rarely accepted my calls. My experience with Jacobson's, an upscale Michigan store chain was typical.

After repeated telephone calls, I finally reached the buyer's assistant, who informed me that Jacobson's probably was not interested in carrying Pheromone. That was all I had to hear. The sale begins when the customer says no.

I immediately drafted a letter to the buyer telling her that I had heard about her fine reputation and I looked forward to meeting her personally. I detailed how hard I had worked to develop my beautiful fragrance and would be privileged to be associated with her organization, then had the letter delivered via messenger.

A few days later, I delivered a sample of Pheromone tied to a bouquet of balloons. In the attached note I wrote, "You are about to experience Pheromone, the world's most precious perfume. I hope you will enjoy it as much as I have enjoyed creating it. I shall call you tomorrow to arrange an appointment."

My bold approach worked. The buyer agreed to meet with me. Midway through my presentation, she interrupted and said, "You don't have to continue, Ms. Miglin. I look forward to working with you."

While my fragrance continued to sell very well at Marshall Field's and other stores, I dreamed of Pheromone taking its rightful place of prestige in the fragrance department of Saks Fifth Avenue. My idea was to open Pheromone at the Saks store in Chicago and prove myself there. As a top model, I had worked many fashion shows at Saks Fifth Avenue as well as doing informal modeling there, which gave me the opportunity to meet everyone at the store.

If I could penetrate the buying offices at Saks' corporate headquarters in New York to secure distribution in the Chicago store, I was confident that my sales would prove to the national buyers that Pheromone was worthy of inclusion in their other stores.

Around this time, in 1980, *Women's Wear Daily* published a stellar feature story about the growing success of Pheromone, adding to my cache of favorable press and publicity. It was this story that helped me secure a meeting with the fragrance buyer in New York.

One particularly scorching day in August, I traveled to Saks' buying offices for a 10 a.m. appointment. At 10:10 a.m., I nervously glanced at my watch, struggling to suppress my anticipation. At 10:20 a.m., that anxiety grew.

Shortly after 10:30, I was ushered into the buyer's tiny, cramped office space. I knew that I was in for a rough time when she greeted me with, "Nobody knows who you are. What's this Pheromone Gold Dust? It sounds like a household cleaner."

I described the success of Pheromone in not only the Chicago market, but throughout the rest of the country as well and said, "I would very much like to open Pheromone in just one of your stores, Chicago, and prove to you that people like my product."

"Well," she snorted, "I personally don't think it's worth it, but since you do have some business in the industry, I suppose that I should present this to my divisional merchandise manager. Come back at 4:30 this afternoon."

I graciously thanked her for her time and agreed to return that afternoon. Exiting the Saks offices, I was a bundle of nerves. My tension was nearly as unbearable as the searing heat. I looked across Forty-Ninth Street to Fifth Avenue; St. Patrick's Cathedral rose before me like a shining beacon and I hurried toward it through the heavy heat and humidity.

There, I spent the next five hours lighting candles and on my knees, praying that Saks Fifth Avenue would take my product.

At 4:30 that afternoon, I returned to the buying headquarters, where I was ushered into another suffocatingly small office with no air conditioning. The divisional merchandise manager was clearly irritable due to the heat. Nervously, I sat on the very edge of my chair.

"We probably have to take your product," she began, "because you're already in some stores."

My heart leaped.

"But," she continued, "You're getting only one store— New York. If you don't sell-through in one month, you're out."

One might think that I would have been dancing on air, but this could not have been further from reality. I was actually devastated.

The New York market is brutal; it was a big place and a big store for this lady and her perfume. Had I been given the opportunity to enter Saks Fifth Avenue through their Chicago store, things would have been much easier.

How would I manage to sell-through in one month when I was still relatively unknown in New York?

Saks placed their order later that month and it was shipped in November, just in time for the holiday season. I thought it best to schedule an in-store appearance the first week of its launch to personally share my enthusiasm and passion with Saks' customers, but still felt apprehensive about my success there.

In the meantime, I had heard of a couple named Pigene and Molly who had been in the radio industry for over fifty years. They broadcast a highly-rated midnight talk show every evening from their apartment on Park Avenue.

Since I had nothing to lose and everything to gain, I took it upon myself to call them and said, "I've heard wonderful things about your special radio show and thought that your listeners might be interested if you will have me as a guest."

"Do you like animals?" was the strange response I received.

"I love animals," I began, "I just love them! I have a dog and other ... "

I never even had a chance to finish my sentence.

"Write this address down, sister," said the gruff voice, "and be here at exactly five minutes to midnight—not before and not after." The man then abruptly clicked off.

Lee was certainly not about to let me go to wandering around New York that late unaccompanied. At precisely five minutes to midnight we rang the doorbell and were buzzed into a little inner vestibule where we stood for exactly four minutes. When another buzzer opened the next door, we ascended a flight of stairs to the appropriate apartment.

To my great surprise, we were greeted by a shoeless man with a cigar, dressed in a tattered robe. He looked like Groucho Marx.

"Are you the one who likes animals?"

"Yes, I like them very much." I hesitated.

"Come on in."

And with that he swung open the door to reveal an apartment crammed with old newspapers, magazines, periodicals, and goodness knows what else. Every corner, every shelf, and every table was littered with paper, leaving no room to navigate freely.

"Find a place," said Pigene's wife Molly to Lee, who maintained his composure and attempted to find a clutter-free area where he could sit.

Then she turned to me. Gesturing to a table with a large ribbon microphone, she said, "You sit here, honey."

Pigene, plopped himself down next to me, puffing away on his cigar, the smoke hanging heavily in the air. I struggled to center myself and emulate Lee's composure when from out of nowhere—an enormous tomcat leapt to the top of the table directly in front of me, his tail switching wildly across my nose.

To say that I jumped in surprise would be an understatement.

"Hey, I thought you liked animals," Pigene said, narrowing his gaze. "Listen, sister, I don't think you're going to be on very long. In fact, I'm going to introduce you and then get you the hell out of here. I don't know anything about perfume anyway."

So I took a deep breath, the cat's tail still swishing from side to side, and Pigene introduced me to his radio audience.

"We've got some broad here tonight, ladies and gentlemen. She's sort of in the perfume industry, but I don't know much about her, he growled. "She's going to talk to you."

"You know, I do want to tell all of you that I like animals very much, and that my products contain no animal ingredients," were the first words from that slipped from my mouth. "I do wish to share with you, this evening, my very special perfume called Pheromone."

I glanced nervously at Pigene, who was leaning back in his chair, nonplussed. Obviously, he did not intend to stop me and so I continued to share the story of my quest for a unique new fragrance.

"Ladies," I said, "this product contains Seven Sacred Oils, documented on ancient papyrus; each of them will stimulate a different behavioral response. Spikenard will stimulate psychic powers. Fo-Ti-Tieng is a sexual stimulant, and you will experience a heightened sense of awareness and pleasure."

At the mention of this, the phone next to Pigene began to ring. Then another line rang and another. In a matter of moments, every one of Pigene and Molly's telephone lines were lit—besieged with listeners who were enthralled with the story of my adventures in creating the perfect perfume.

Molly looked at Pigene, who just shrugged and my scheduled five minute interview turned into a two-hour question and answer session.

Lee and I returned to our hotel room after two in the morning. He kissed me and told me what a fine job I had done, and I collapsed in bed, completely exhausted.

When I arrived at Saks the next morning for my personal appearance, I could hardly believe my eyes! Outside the store was a line of people stretching through the doors all the way to the cosmetics counter inside—the result of my radio appearance the night before. Each of these customers could not wait

At a department store personal appearance

to meet me and to experience Pheromone, which sold out at Saks within days.

The rest is history. Eventually, Pheromone was launched in not only *every* Saks Fifth Avenue store, but in other luxury department and specialty stores across the country, including Neiman Marcus, Nordstrom, Lord & Taylor, Bloomingdale's, and Bergdorfs.

Several years later, while brainstorming new in-store promotions for Pheromone, which by then had become a top-five selling brand, I revisited my books on the ancient art of perfumery. There, still pressed between two pages, I rediscovered a gift bestowed upon me by a mysterious old man in Egypt—a small, weathered feather.

Holding it between my fingers, I closed my eyes and briefly relived my quest to develop a fragrance unlike no other, understanding with certainty that it had indeed been my destiny.

The reappearance of that special gift also gave me a wonderful idea for an in-store sampling promotion, which I called "Pheromone is in the air." Rather than using the traditional manner of spraying my perfume on a paper blotter card, the promotion enjoyed great success by using scented feathers, which department store customers tucked into their purses before resuming their shopping.

Later, when the ladies opened their purse in search of wallet or car keys, the scent of Pheromone rose upward to entice them. Women loved the feathers, which helped to remind them of my beautiful fragrance, which they also loved.

Although feathers would later play another important role in my life, that particular quill, so meaningful to me, still lies pressed between the same two pages of my special book—a constant reminder of memories shared and dreams fulfilled.

CHAPTER FIVE

"The human soul needs actual beauty even more than it needs bread."

How you feel about yourself and your self-esteem is by far the most important aspect of beauty.

Any plastic surgeon can tell you stories of lives being completely changed following a minor surgical procedure. It is the renewal of that patient's self-confidence that makes the difference in her life, rather than the surgery itself.

I discovered this fact one afternoon in 1979 when a young woman entered my Oak Street Institute.

Shrouded in a dark scarf wrapped about her head, the woman's face was hidden by dark glasses. She nervously paced the floor of the salon looking around, then abruptly turned and walked out.

Always concerned with any potential customer's first reaction upon entering my salon, I excused myself from the client with whom I was working. I stepped out from behind the makeup station, followed her outside, and introduced myself.

"Hello, I'm Marilyn Miglin," I said, extending my hand. She paused briefly to look at me from behind her sunglasses, and reluctantly raised a gloved hand.

"Michelle McBride."

"I'm terribly sorry that there was no one available to assist you," I apologized. "Please come back inside. As soon as I have finished with my customer, I shall be happy to work with you."

"No, I don't think you could possibly help me," she said shaking her head. "Not looking the way I do."

Before I could respond, she reached up and removed her scarf and glasses, revealing a face completely covered with thick red scar tissue.

I stood there dumbfounded.

Everything around me seemed to stand still as I looked at her. My reaction was not one of horror or repulsion, but rather surprise. I did not know what to say.

Sensing my hesitation, she re-tied her scarf, adjusted her sunglasses, and turned on the sidewalk to leave.

"Please," I said, "I can help you. If you would just come back with me and wait until I finish with my customer, we can talk. It would be my pleasure to work with you."

Michelle regarded me with caution, but I felt that she needed to trust someone—me or anyone else who may have been able to offer her some assistance.

"Come back inside," I said. "I'll get you some coffee and as soon as I have finished with my client, we'll talk."

She looked at me, then at the salon door, and finally nodded yes, following me back up the stairs into the salon, where I helped to make her comfortable in a private area.

Returning to my original client, I could not help but think about Michelle. When I brought her some coffee, I noticed she was glancing up at the ceiling of the salon which was adorned with white clouds.

For some reason, I felt a strong connection and was anxious to speak with her. I wished very much to help her, although I was unsure of exactly how I would do so.

I certainly had no intention of treating her any differently than any other client. Yet, I could not possibly begin to imagine what had caused such traumatic scarring, or what it was that had ultimately brought her to my salon.

When we finally sat down together, she told me her story. I learned more than I ever wanted to know.

As a child, Michelle had attended the Our Lady of the Angels parish school in Chicago. One December afternoon in 1958, one of the worst fires in the city's history swept through the school. Within minutes, twelve-hundred students were scrambling for their lives, many leaping from windows to escape the inferno. Ninety-two children and three nuns were killed. Scores of others were injured.

In its aftermath, the fire ushered in new laws to protect Illinois school children. It also left Michelle with scar tissue over much of her face, hands, and body.

Just twelve-years old at the time, Michelle carried three children from the inferno. Not realizing that her own flesh was on fire, she kept returning to the building to rescue smaller children.

When she regained consciousness in a hospital room, she heard the voice of her father speaking with a doctor. In hushed tones, the doctor sighed, "It would be better if she dies."

For the next ten years in burn and psychiatric wards, she struggled to find any semblance of normality. What no one realized was that although modern medicine had indeed saved her life and kept her functioning physically, she had no zest for living.

I was devastated while I listened to her story. Anyone could have been in that fire.

With Michelle now sitting comfortably before me in a private room, I was confident that I would be able to help her feel better about her appearance. I arranged before me various foundations, powders, and specialized products I used for models.

As I worked, she shared with me the humiliation and hurt she had endured as a teenager when thoughtless people talked about her and taunted her with names as though she could not hear them. As an adult, Michelle had found it increasingly difficult to face social situations and to meet new people, let alone obtain a job. As a result, her expectations and opportunities were limited, and she found it easier to withdraw than to reach out to others.

Confidently, I mixed together several colors and began gently applying foundation to her face, but to my surprise it all slid off.

I tried another, and it too slipped off the slick scar tissue.

Finally, I mixed together powder with foundation, creating a tackier substance, which did adhere somewhat and left a slightly better appearance—for the first time, she smiled. But, I knew surely there had to be something more that I could do for her.

"Let me work with my chemist," I offered, "to formulate something else for you."

In the meantime, she did gain some confidence in what I was able to do and at least left the salon without covering her face with her scarf.

Perhaps she sensed in me a sincerity she had been unaccustomed to. I only know that there had to be a special reason for my meeting her. Undoubtedly, it was a higher power that guided Michelle McBride into my salon that day and recognizing this made me even more determined to accept the challenge of finding a solution to her needs.

Dr. Fiedler worked diligently to isolate any ingredients that would adhere to scar tissue. Adding more binding agents, he reformulated my foundation. Then I took over to experiment with this newly created makeup. Although it did adhere to scar tissue, sponging it on did not create the natural look I desired. It took practice and a lot of ad-libbing, but finally I developed an effective technique by using a stippling effect with the foundation, forming a skin-like texture over scars.

Three weeks later I telephoned Michelle and asked her to return.

We chose the best of Dr. Fiedler's three prototypes and she could not have been more thrilled with the results. As she began to learn how to apply her own makeup, she gained even more self-esteem, confiding in me that she no longer felt the desire to commit suicide. She finally began letting a higher power guide her.

Eventually, Michelle gained enough courage to ask me to allow her to work as an intern at the salon for one year, adding that if I truly felt that she looked as good as I indicated to her, I should have no hesitations in having my customers see her.

She did go on to work with me, finally writing the book, *The Fire That Would Not Die.* She ceased living in the past, embraced the future and ultimately decided that she would use her own life experience to help others in situations similar to her own.

Creating her own network of support, Michelle reached out to communicate with other burn survivors, sharing her time and considerable energy with the American Red Cross and Chicago's Cook County Hospital Burn Unit. She also founded a support group which she called the Phoenix Foundation, after the mythical bird rising renewed from the ashes.

Unexpectedly, a few months later, I received a call from Cook County Hospital, asking if I might consider working with several burn survivors. Michelle had recommended me.

How could I say no? I considered the request an honor.

I must admit that the Burn Unit administrators were skeptical. Michelle's enthusiasm had made an impact on them, but they were still unclear as to what I could do to provide these burn survivors with renewed hope. The doctors were interested in how I could help the patients feel better about themselves and their lives after surgery, grafting, and physical therapy had been completed.

Since I had some doubts myself, I enlisted the assistance of my creative director, Camylle DeLaurentis. We discussed in detail how best to work with these patients. I had learned a great deal from working with Michelle, but I had also established an emotional bond with her that had helped both of us reach a positive outcome. Working at the hospital would be a totally new experience.

I decided that Camylle and I needed to drastically alter our own appearance. Since we would be working in a hospital, rather than my salon, I felt that it was important for us to blend into this environment in order to create a level of trust.

We removed our jewelry, our bright nail polish and our red lipstick. Then we donned white lab coats. To soften any skepticism from the initial patients we were scheduled to see that day, we asked to be introduced as "color and texture technicians," rather than makeup designers. Our task we felt was to restore both pigment and texture to scarred skin. Since I am tall, I also insisted upon being seated before a patient was brought in to see me.

My first visit to the Cook County Hospital Burn Unit was not what I had expected. I had assumed that we would work with several burn survivors in the comfort of a private office. Instead, when we arrived at the hospital, we were guided down the hallways of the emergency burn unit, complete with its background of agonized screams and the moans of patients who had only just arrived for treatment.

Camylle's eyes widened in apprehension, as did mine. I was no longer in the comfort zone of my own beautiful salon.

Initially, we met with three patients, each of whom was wearing custom-made elastic garments, called Jobsts. The pressure from the elastic modified scar tissue to reduce the formation of keloids and hypertrophic scarring. Wrapped in this elastic, the patients presented a reasonably normal appearance, with only a hint of any tissue damage underneath. Without the Jobsts, however, the burn scars were exposed and the extent of the trauma was very evident.

I had been warned that convincing patients to remove their Jobsts would be difficult. It would be a matter of winning their trust. They had to believe that we could help them. The white lab coats and our professional demeanor helped a little, but they were both quiet and suspicious.

I began with the first patient by asking for her trust in allowing me to demonstrate exactly what I could do to improve the appearance of one of her scarred hands.

Stippling and smoothing on a new texture, I worked as swiftly as I could. She sat perfectly still watching me. Transfixed at the results, she raised her hands in front of her to admire them.

Suddenly, she began to pour out her feelings, sharing with me how she longed for a more normal appearance.

"Let's see what we can do with this area," I said as casually as I could, indicating some scar tissue on the left side of her face.

"You have beautiful eyes," I complimented her. "Let's downplay the scar tissue here and emphasize them, which is where people should be looking."

She relaxed a bit and nodded, indicating her willingness to allow me to work on her face. As I worked, she continued to share her feelings concerning her appearance.

And so began the development of my method in working with the facially disfigured. The routine rarely varies.

The first challenge is always to help patients overcome their initial apprehension, offering a glimmer of hope that they can feel better about their appearance. That has always been the most difficult task. Without that trust, the patient is not open to other possibilities.

Another challenge was in working with African-Americans. The scar tissue from burns on light-colored skin is not nearly as drastic as that of darker complexions. Darker skin that has been burned has a loss of pigmentation, resulting in milky white lesions, with white and pink scar tissue contrasting vividly against the skin's natural color. Restoration of an even pigmentation was enough to bring new hope to these survivors, allowing them to feel a semblance of normalcy again.

The end of that first day in the Burn Unit brought stunning results. The patients, the program administrators, and certainly Camylle and I felt that we had made a difference.

Over the course of the next year or so, we continued to meet with patients at the Burn Unit, showing them how they could use makeup to improve their self-image and self-confidence. Some of the scarring is horrific, but we do the best we can to help everyone, and when the patients learn to apply makeup properly, their appearance is often dramatically changed for the better.

Like Michelle, once they know they look better, their confidence returns.

Often times, the hospital would refer patients to the salon as well, where we worked with them in a private room to lessen their emotional discomfort. We did our best to ensure that they all left feeling much better about themselves.

Word of mouth regarding our work with burn survivors continued to spread, and before long, other people with varying degrees of scarring and pigmentation problems, such as vitiligo and lupus, came to the salon.

One customer named Marilyn walked in one day with the worst case of psoriasis I had ever seen. Everyone in the salon who saw her was repulsed, and of course, she immediately picked up on this.

"I suppose you're like everybody else. None of you want to touch me," she said.

That was all I had to hear. I smiled at her and said, "Of course I'll touch you."

Using my undercover, I began gently press-patting the areas of her affected skin. Not only was she overwhelmed with my touch, but the undercover balanced her skin tone and her condition became much less apparent.

Over the years, she sang my praises at Northwestern Memorial Hospital, and eventually the dermatologists there began using my products. Her daughter, Faith, also became a loyal customer.

Then, on a very cold January morning, over ten years ago, I received a call from Dr. Susan Habakuk at the University of Illinois Craniofacial Center for Anomalies.

"You don't know me, but I have heard about you and your work with burn survivors," she said. "I also know that you have worked at the Cook County Burn Unit. The Craniofacial Center, where I am located, is a comprehensive treatment facility.

145

Rather than making our patients travel from one location to another to see many different specialists, each individual we treat at the Center may see all their doctors and therapists in one place.

"We recognize your reputation as a cosmetic specialist, Mrs. Miglin, and we wonder if you . . ." she hesitated.

"Many of the patients here live with severe craniofacial abnormalities," Susan continued slowly. "Most of them are dealing with more than scar tissue caused by burns. They appear noticeable for many reasons. Cleft palates, craniofacial conditions such as Crouzon's Syndrome, other birth defects, and cancer have robbed them of 'normal' appearances."

I listened to her with interest, wondering what she was leading up to.

"Medical treatment and plastic surgery can help, but it cannot cure a condition completely. Treatment may also continue for many years and living with a face or body which is different from everyone else's is not easy," she said.

"I understand that," I answered. "Stares, comments, and questions are difficult to deal with."

"Yes," she said. "It can be devastating for these patients. How can they feel good about themselves when looks seem to count for so much?"

"What can I do to help them?"

"We would like to enlist your expertise as an experiment," said Susan. "Although standard treatments can make a big difference to someone's appearance, some disfigurement often remains. Adults with disfigurements can find it difficult to deal with social situations, meet strangers, make friends, or even get a job. Often they find it easier to withdraw from social contact altogether. Many of these patients are prone to suicide.

"We follow these patients throughout their entire medical program, but there comes a time when all methods of treatment are finally exhausted and there is nothing more we can do. At that point, these patients are on their own, as cold as that may sound," she sighed.

"So these people find themselves struggling to re-enter society," I said, understanding completely what she was saying, as so many of the burn survivors I had already worked with had experienced similar circumstances.

Susan went on. "We would like for you to visit the center and allow us to introduce you to the staff and some of our patients. That would be the first step. If you feel comfortable, we'd like to see if your work can help them achieve a smoother transition when they leave the Center.

"To be honest, Mrs. Miglin," she said, "we've already interviewed a dozen cosmetologists and paramedical professionals from all over the country and have not yet found someone who understands how to treat our patients. No one seems to be able to handle the severity of the cases we see here."

For me, working at the Craniofacial Center was not a difficult decision to make. It was something I felt compelled to do. Remember, I am a girl who cannot say, "no."

And so one frigid morning in January, Camylle and I took a taxi to the University of Illinois at Chicago campus. We entered a stately, turn-of-the-century building and there we met Susan, who greeted us warmly. After a tour of the facility and an introduction to several doctors on the staff, we adjourned to Susan's office where she pulled several medical books from her shelves. They contained color photographs of trauma patients.

We looked at graphic photos of children with Crouzon's Syndrome, cleft palettes, and port wine birth marks, and adults with facial prosthetics including artificial noses, ears, and entire sections of their faces—each case the result of accidents, chemical burns, cancer, and repeated surgery. Susan slowly turned the pages of the books, gauging our reactions.

Camylle sat rigidly in her chair and I could barely speak. It was not that I found the photos of these patients horrifying. Rather, I was at a loss to understand what I could do for them. Working with my specialized makeup formulations on burn survivors and individuals suffering the loss of color from vitiligo was about creating renewed texture and restoring pigmentation. This was not the same thing at all.

And yet, Susan and the staff impressed me greatly. I felt as though somehow, we could indeed assist these patients in some way and even teach the medical community something about what I already knew—that cosmetics can play a positive role in altering physical and mental health.

After conferring with Camylle, I said, "Of course we'll try to help."

"Wonderful." Susan smiled. We had obviously passed her test. "It will be trial and error," she cautioned.

"Isn't that what life is all about?" I said. "It will be a discovery process for all of us. We'll learn as we go."

We said good-bye to Susan and stepped into a taxi. As the cab headed north to the salon, Camylle and I sat in silence for a long time before I finally asked, "What do you think?"

She turned to me and sighed, "What do I think? I've worked with you for seventeen years now and I show up not knowing exactly what any day will bring. Working with you is like being shot out of cannon, Marilyn. I never know where we will land."

She paused for a moment and then said, "We'll do it."

Of course, Camylle was correct. I have never lived life in the past nor worried about the future. I take every day as it comes and try to make it an adventure.

Over the next few months, Camylle and I read as much as we could about facial trauma and enrolled in classes that taught how best to deal with patients and their families. Our training also included learning as much as we could about all the treatments offered by the Center.

Since there was not a vacant room at the Craniofacial Center from which we could work, we scheduled our first consultation on a Friday afternoon, because all of the doctors were away at their weekly meeting.

Finally the day arrived when I met my first patient, a young woman with a cleft palate named Peggy Ryan. She entered the room, sat down, and never once lifted her head so that I could see her face.

"I suppose you are going to tell me I have on a pretty dress," she mumbled without looking up.

"Well, I wasn't going to, but if you'd like me to comment on your dress, Peggy, I shall."

"That's what all the doctors say."

"Actually, you and I are here to do something that the doctors have never done. They have asked me here to help improve the quality of life for their patients after all the surgeries are over. Perhaps if you and I work together, you can help me open some new avenues of understanding for other patients."

I asked her to look up at me, so that I could see her. She looked up briefly and then down again.

"Why, you have beautiful blue eyes, Peggy," I said. "Have you ever worn makeup?"

"No. No one has ever told me that before."

"Let's work to enhance and make them even more noticeable for everyone to admire. Shall I show you how?"

Reluctantly she agreed, but kept her hand over her mouth.

I was determined to stress the positive with Peggy, because that is the only way that one gains the confidence and trust of another person. I applied makeup to one of her eyes and then handed her a mirror.

"There. Now doesn't it look twice as big?" I asked.

When she agreed, I continued, "We are going to create the most beautiful blue eyes that anyone will ever see. Then, no matter who you meet, they will comment them. You will look and feel like a different person."

Handing her a brush, I said, "Now I want you to do the other one"

"No, I can't do that." She shook her head. "I don't know how."

"I'm going to teach you. You'll be able to go home and do it in five minutes. Really."

After teaching her to put makeup on her other eye, I progressively worked on more of her face, creating a high cheekbone and adding a little foundation to smooth out her skin. I was now near her mouth, so I said, "I know that you are sensitive about your uneven lip-line, Peggy, but what would you say if I told you that I can create a very natural one with my theatrical pencil?"

"How do you know I don't have a lip-line?"

"I have worked with your condition before," I explained patiently.

Reluctantly she dropped her hand from her mouth.

This was the critical moment.

Using a wax-based pencil, I carefully followed the natural line of her lower lip, then the top, continuing over the area distorted by the scarring, using short, deft strokes, as though it did not exist. I delicately sponged new texture around the scar tissue and filled in her lips with a natural gloss. Lipstick would have been too much for her to accept due to the fact that she was always trying to cover this part of her face with her hand. When I finished, I asked her to look in the mirror.

She suddenly sat up straighter and smiled. "How did you do that? I have a lip line! It looks so natural!"

"You look lovely," I complimented her.

She continued to stare at her reflection.

"You can barely tell that I have a scar," she marveled. "Will you teach me how you did that?"

I proceeded to teach her how to do so.

When Susan returned to the office to say good-bye to Peggy, she was amazed at the results, both cosmetically and emotionally. My protégé had a new aura of confidence. She fluttered her eyes at Susan, explaining how she had learned to line them with color and definition.

"And how do you feel about the scar?" Susan cautiously asked.

"You can hardly see it! It's seems to have disappeared"

One stipulation I required, which the clinic still maintains, is that patients return on a monthly basis. When Peggy returned for her next appointment, her hair was permed, she was wearing a new suit, and she was walking with assurance. She had just landed her first job and I could not have been more delighted for her.

Interestingly, I saw her again just recently, and she shared with me that she had found a new boyfriend, bought a house, and was enjoying a quality of life that she never thought she could attain.

That was the way it all began. At first I worked with minor cases, such as Peggy, and then cautiously worked my way up to those with more severe problems. Always I involved the person with whom I was working—consulting with them first about what they felt were their most positive physical attributes. Once we enhanced the positive, drawing attention away from the affected area of the face, we then worked to make other areas less noticeable.

I went on to visit the clinic every month for many years and saw the same wonderful changes in both personality and confidence which Peggy had experienced in patient after patient. The people whom I have been fortunate enough to work with at the Craniofacial Center have each reached out for a new life.

As time went on, the doctors began to notice the positive psychological changes that a little makeup brought to their patients. They were absolutely amazed at how a little makeup could affect the healing process and noticed a marked change in depression and suicide attempts.

Most importantly, the doctors began to notice their patients smiling, something they had never done before during the treatment process.

With Marlena and a young patient at the Craniofacial Center

One African-American teenager had been born with Crouzon's Syndrome. Her facial features were misaligned, and by the time I met her, she had endured forty-one surgeries—each time the surgeon opened her skull in order to move her eyes forward into a more normal position. Her dark skin had developed hundreds of white scars which were quite apparent on her otherwise lovely complexion.

Merely covering this young girl's scars with makeup sparked a major emotional breakthrough for her. I also arranged to have her fitted for new glasses, softening the uneven appearance of her eyes and her severe hairstyle. From being a "D" student, she went on to receive all "A's," and proudly attended her first prom with a new boyfriend.

I have always taken great joy in working with children. Often times, their parents proved to be more challenging than the young patients. Naturally, they want only the best for their own child, but cannot always see clearly how their own actions affect them.

The scars on one young girl noticeably distorted her skin tone. She was only thirteen, and not really interested in makeup. All she wanted was for her skin to look even and normal so that others would not stare at her scars. When I successfully camouflaged them, her face lit up with pleasure.

Then her mother said, "Now how about some lipstick? Can you make her look like. . ."

I try my best to convince parents to wait in another room, so I may gain their child's trust and free myself to work with them properly.

The most challenging case I encountered was a New Guinea woman with leprosy. She had contracted it in her native country over twenty years earlier, and because of the disease, her husband had left her. The Craniofacial Center was her last hope.

I was not worried about the danger of contagion and so I had no particular apprehensions about working with her. Susan had cautioned me that the skin of those with this disease turned silver in color, but I was not overly concerned. I was sure that she was talking about gray or muddy-looking tones.

The day of our appointment, I donned a medical body suit, booties, and a double set of surgical gloves, which were taped to the suit, as well as a face mask and goggles. I felt like an astronaut, but the medical staff insisted upon taking no chances.

With great confidence, I entered the consultation to meet my patient.

And her skin *was* silver.

Struggling to maintain my composure, my mind raced ahead to what colors would create an entirely new skin tone. I suddenly realized that I would need every shade of the spectrum.

Finally, after creating a color formulation as best I could with the supplies I had brought with me, I gently dipped my sponge into the foundation and carefully reached out to apply it to her nose.

To my horror, her nose caved in.

Later I found out that the bone structure had been eaten away over the years by the leprosy and each time I touched her skin, it collapsed as if it were a down pillow.

What does one say in a situation like this?

"Does that hurt?" was all I could offer.

"No," she replied, shrugging, as her children stood behind me watching every move of the sponge as I stippled away.

When I finally corrected the silver tone of her skin, she wept openly.

"Now I wish to go out and have men admire me. I feel like a woman again," she said.

Perhaps one of the most rewarding experiences I enjoyed was in working with a young man named Larry, who arrived for his appointment with a baseball hat worn backward, his head held very low.

Susan explained that he had been badly burned in an automobile accident, destroying nearly all the cartilage of both his ears. Although tissue-paper thin, the small vestiges that remained were extremely important to Larry and were something in which he took great pride. At least he still had them.

Unfortunately, one day while being lowered into a therapeutic pool, a technician accidentally hit Larry's ears, literally knocking off what had remained.

Devastated, he began to cry, displaying primal emotions unknown to the therapists who worked with him. As the months progressed, Susan Habakuk created for Larry a pair of prosthetic ears—so lifelike that no one would ever suspect that they were not real.

Larry's emotional scars still remained, however, and his sensitivity to the uneven scar tissue on the back of his head bordered on obsessive. No matter where he was, he refused to remove his baseball hat, even though his hair now covered much of it.

One day, he told me that he had been invited to a wedding but did not feel that he could attend, fearing that it would be most inappropriate for him not to remove his hat in church.

"You're right," I said. "People are only going to wonder why you don't take it off and ask what happened to you."

I continued to work with him over the months but one day, I finally said, "This is it. I want you to take that hat off, Larry. You and I are going to go outside, walk around the block and we're going to see who looks at your head. I have been coming here to see you for a long time now and you owe me one thing, and that is to remove that hat."

Reluctantly, he did so and we went outside.

No one even looked at me, much less Larry.

"There! You see," I said. "Nobody stopped. Nobody looked. Nobody said or did anything.

Larry left the clinic that day without his hat and since then has moved forward with his life. The last time I saw him, he visited not for a scheduled appointment, but to say thank you, giving me that tightest bear hug I think I have ever received. I knew then how much his self-confidence had meant to him.

As my involvement at the Center continued to evolve over the next five years, I was disappointed that at first none of the doctors ever took the time to meet me. Until, that is, they began to recognize significant changes taking place in their patients—patients who no longer expressed a desire to commit suicide, patients who seemed to enjoy increased confidence and were progressing more rapidly.

One day, all of the doctors waited for me to finish working with a patient to express their appreciation and congratulations. After seeing such positive results in the smiles and increased confidence in their patients, the medical staff asked students in the University of Illinois' medical arts and dermatology departments to observe our work. I was thrilled to have been able to expand the knowledge and awareness of such a group of people.

But when the Craniofacial Center invited me to join its staff as their only nonmedical professional, I truly felt honored.

News of my work spread throughout Chicago, and the more I was interviewed in the newspapers, and on TV and radio, the more attention it garnered for the Center. As people became aware of the brilliant work being done by the University's dedicated team of professionals, others began to volunteer their time, and donations began to trickle in.

As time went on, the Clinic recognized the work I was doing, and today, there is a plaque with my name on a wall. More importantly, I helped form an advisory board, whose fund-rais-

ing efforts have aided the completion of a new five-million dollar facility for the Craniofacial Center.

In life, things somehow come together if you open yourself
to each opportunity that comes your way.

One day, Nena Ivon, fashion director at Saks Fifth Avenue
asked to see me. We had been close friends for many years, but
given the formality of her call, I could not imagine what it was
she wished to discuss. To my surprise, Nena informed me that
the Fashion Group, for which I had previously established a
scholarship fund for aspiring young designers, wished to recognize my contributions by giving me their "Woman of the Year"
award.

Although I was touched by this gesture, I politely declined,
explaining that the purpose of my philanthropic work was not
so that I could be honored at a gala award dinner.

"But you're such a positive role model," Nena enthused.
"Surely there must be a charity which could utilize the benefits
generated by your acceptance of this award."

After careful consideration, I decided to accept that first
award and earmarked the proceeds for the Clinic, which had
few funds available for special needs. Moreover, I hated the bil-
ious green of the walls which both the patients and staff found
depressing.

Joan Blutter, a member of both the Fashion Group Board
and the American Society of Interior Designers, offered her
organization's support to paint the walls of the Clinic. A Viet-
nam refugee, happy he was now an American citizen,
volunteered to create a mural. As each person reached out, others became involved, and together, we made a difference.

Accepting the Fashion Group Award

That which we consider to be beautiful is subjective. The Venus de Milo has no arms. Yet, she is considered to be an example of beauty by which we measure ourselves, even today.

Today, when anyone asks me of my greatest accomplishment in life, I always refer back to the Craniofacial Center—not the patients necessarily, but the doctors. The fact that the medical community now recognizes the importance of makeup for the self esteem of their patients remains both my proudest achievement and the sweetest reward I could ever enjoy.

In the end, when the doctors have done all they can—I am the one who has the pleasure of painting the prettiest picture.

CHAPTER SIX

*L*ee Miglin believed in big dreams. It was his vision to create the highest-identity, highest quality, highest-profile office buildings in Chicago. Why was it, he wondered, that it was developers from other cities who were the ones already doing this? Why were these other developers being imported?

At that time, Arthur Rubloff & Co. was going through some dramatic changes. Many of those who had founded the company and made it a success were either retiring or passing away. Rubloff began to take on a new focus—more corporate service oriented rather than entrepreneurial.

Lee felt he was better suited for creating his own company rather than continuing in the new direction Rubloff was taking and so, in 1982, he founded Miglin-Beitler Development. His first endeavor was a magnificent building, called Madison Plaza, which was leased by the Hyatt Corporation. Nearly overnight, his new development company was heralded as a success. He continued with President's Plaza III near O'Hare Airport, the largest,

With Lee at the topping out ceremony for Madison Plaza

single contiguous development outside Chicago's Loop. He then followed that with Oakbrook Terrace, a stunning property that remains the tallest building in the Midwest outside of Chicago and is now considered a landmark.

If you were to walk into any of Lee's properties and looked around, you would feel as if the building had just opened that day. Striving to offer the most exceptional service possible, he created a management company built on the simple premise that the tenant is always right. As a result, he established a reputation for his own properties that drew interest from other corporations who asked him to manage their buildings as well.

It was Lee's philosophy that upon the anniversary of every lease, a bottle of Dom Perignon be presented to the head of the office to thank him for being a tenant. His management style was both impeccable and inspiring.

He also established a firm commitment to the art community with each of his new developments. For many years, he felt the arts were cherished and enjoyed by only the wealthiest. In order for most people to have any experience with art, it required at a visit to a museum or gallery.

Lee believed that it was his civic responsibility to promote public art in a manner that others could not. For each new building he developed, he commissioned sculptures and art pieces from American artists, displaying them in a manner that would enrich a person's work day in a way that could not otherwise be provided in that environment.

Jerry Peart, whose sculpture was to grace the President's Plaza, asked Lee, "How big can I make the piece?"

"What is your dream, Jerry?" answered Lee. "Make it as big as you wish. I want you to make your dream a reality."

He hired Nancy Graves to produce the largest piece of art she had ever created for the lobby of his Oakbrook Terrace skyscraper. The twenty-two-foot tall nickel alloy sculpture was absolutely spectacular and I was so proud. No other contributor, bank, or business had ever put together the array of masterpiece sculpture that Lee had.

Lee opened each new building with an extravagant flourish. He titled one grand opening party "Blue Geisha," and arranged for the servers to be dressed as geishas. Permanently installed artwork was then unveiled in the same theme.

He commissioned a work from Louise Nevelson, the first woman sculptor in Chicago with an international following. Louise loved the distinctive lines of a building Lee was developing on Wells Street, and the energy of the passing el trains. The building, featuring these dramatic shadows, opened with the theme "Dawn Shadows." Louise's sculpture with the same name was unveiled to much fanfare, with thousands of black and white balloons being released into the sky.

It was said that people immediately recognized a Lee Miglin building by simply looking at the walls, the interior, the elevators, the floors, the cleanliness, the artwork, and the flowers—all impeccable and identifiable traits.

Lee loved to do things the right way. He was full of loving detail in everything he did, not only as a formidable developer, but as a devoted husband as well.

As a model, I was constantly exhausting pairs of panty hose and purchasing new ones. On my birthday one year, he presented to me one hundred pair of L'eggs stockings, each still in the little plastic egg in which it was packaged. Every day, I would open another egg to enjoy a fresh pair of hose. One morning, however, when I split open a new plastic egg, I found, in addition to stockings, an exquisite blue star sapphire ring encrusted with diamonds.

"Oh, Lee!" I sighed, suddenly realizing that this wonderful man had been waiting so very patiently for me to open that particular "egg." He was an extraordinary romantic.

On yet another birthday, I came home to find one-thousand roses everywhere in my house.

Meanwhile, I was busy exploring opportunities for the growth of my new fragrance division, traveling the country to promote Pheromone. In city after city, I visited department stores and was interviewed by the press. Both the media and women alike were absolutely mesmerized by the scent and the story of its development.

In New York, I held court with a handful of beauty and fashion editors from *Town & Country, Harper's Bazaar,* and

With Lee, celebrating an anniversary

Cosmopolitan, entertaining them in a palatial luxury suite at the Plaza Hotel.

That morning, while preparing to greet my guests, I accidentally dropped a bottle of Pheromone Bath & Body Oil on the marble floor of the bathroom. The glass bottle shattered and I quickly stooped to clean the fragrant mess before I finished dressing.

After successful interviews with each editor, I packed my luggage and headed back to Chicago. The following morning, I was contacted by the concierge of the Plaza. It seemed that the next occupant of the suite in which I had stayed was creating a fuss in ascertaining the nature of the scent that greeted him in the bathroom where I had spilled my oil.

"What is this wonderful smell?" he demanded. Where could he find it?

With my approval, the Plaza gave this gentleman the telephone number to my office in Chicago, and within minutes he was in contact with me. As fate would have it, he was an Arabian Prince who insisted upon placing a ten thousand dollar order for his harem.

Maintaining a presence in the high-end market was not easy. I had gained entrance and had a foot in the door, but that did mean that I could stay there without proving myself through sales every single day. I managed to stay afloat with a highly personal marketing strategy, making appearances in all of the seven-hundred stores that carried Pheromone.

I also offered constant reinforcement to the eighteen-hundred "line girls," or beauty advisors, who sold my brand at the fragrance counters. Each month, I handwrote a note to every single one of them and answered all their letters. Sometimes I called them if they had done something extraordinarily wonderful, like selling a one-ounce bottle of perfume. I never forgot to say thank-you. I worked the floor alongside them and asked if there was anything I could do to help them improve their sales.

I made sure they had samples and brochures. Never did I forget that these were the women who helped build my business. They were and still are the closest to the customer.

To be sure, traveling to promote Pheromone was always an adventure, but it also involved grueling hours spent aboard airplanes and inside hotels for interviews and appearances. There were many days when I got up at 3:00 a.m., boarded a flight to take me where it was I had to go, and then came home very late at night. Business was important, but of course Lee and the children were more so.

No matter where I was and despite the circumstances, I was adamant about attending to the business at hand and then immediately returning home to my family.

Sometimes, however, this was easier said than done.

After an appearance in Dallas, my creative director Camylle and I trudged back to the airport, eager to beat the rush hour and enjoy dinner with our husbands and children. In those days, it was unusual for gentleman traveling in first-class to find themselves seated next to a lady. It was an unwritten rule that first-class status belonged to the elite businessmen-only club, and on this particular occasion our fellow passengers registered curiosity when we boarded the plane.

Spreading out our paperwork, Camylle and I paid no attention and prepared to discuss the day's business during the flight home. That is, until it was announced that due to mechanical problems, our flight would be indefinitely delayed.

To a seasoned business traveler, any delay which involves being forced to sit trapped aboard a crowded plane on the tarmac is unbearable and this particular occasion was no different. We were quite relieved when the door was opened and the passengers were afforded the opportunity to return to the terminal until the situation was corrected. We were assured that an announcement would be made when the flight was ready to leave, and so Camylle and I deplaned to telephone our families.

Imagine my surprise not twenty minutes later, when through the windows of the terminal, I saw our plane slowly taxiing away. I was incredulous! This was inexcusable—completely unacceptable that we had not been notified of the plane's re-boarding and departure as promised. If I had to take matters into my own hands in order to get back home to my family, I was not above doing so.

As I called for Camylle, who was across the terminal on a pay-phone, an airline employee adorned with a communication headset and microphone passed in front of me near the boarding gate. When it became obvious that he was not about to offer any assistance, I found myself breaking from my normal demeanor and pulling his headset away from him.

Desperate times sometimes call for desperate measures. The poor man gasped in shock when I pulled the earphone and mouthpiece closer to me, thereby dragging him along with it.

"Marilyn! What are you doing!" shouted Camylle, who by then quickly grasped the situation at hand.

"Bring back that plane," I calmly demanded into the headset.

"Lady! You can't do that!" gasped the gate employee.

"You bring that plane back," I repeated. "Bring it back right now."

By now, the commotion had begun to attract unwanted attention at the gate. Camylle was completely mortified—but bring back the airplane they did.

"Thank you very much," I smiled, returning the man's headset. No doubt, this was one disgruntled passenger he would never forget.

"The people on that plane are going to hate us," lamented Camylle, as we walked the jetway to reboard. "I am so embarrassed."

"I don't care," I answered. "It's been a long day and I want to go home."

Her grimace upon entering the bulkhead of the plane, however, brightened considerably when our fellow passengers greeted us with a wild round of applause.

But that was not the end. As I moved down the aisle to my seat, my paperwork was no longer where I had left it.

"Where are my folders?" I inquired impatiently to the flight attendant, who shifted her stance from one foot to the other.

"If you'll just take your seat, ma'am," she said, "I'll find out what happened to your things."

By now, our treatment from this airline had gone too far, and I politely refused to be seated until my paperwork and sales reports were returned to me. Sheepishly, she departed momentarily and returned with a garbage bag, from which my folders were extracted.

If Camylle had been embarrassed earlier, it was now the flight attendant's turn. The pained look on her face as she handed my papers to me confirmed it.

As I took my seat and adjusted my belt for takeoff, a businessman across the aisle leaned over and quietly said, "You've got chutzpah, lady."

"A girl must do what a girl must do," I smiled, before closing my eyes for a much needed nap.

In all these years, I have never missed a planned appearance or an interview and I have never failed to return home. Delayed or cancelled flights can be challenging, but sometimes one's mode of transportation in her own city is equally taxing.

Following another appearance in Seattle, my five-and-a-half hour return flight arrived at O'Hare well past midnight. What I wanted more than anything else was to be delivered to my doorstep, where Lee was waiting, remove my makeup, take a bath, and go to sleep.

The enticing thought of peaceful slumber was apparently shared by the driver whose taxicab I had randomly chosen at the airport. Whether or not he had been driving his cab for eighteen hours, was intoxicated, or suffered from random spells of narcolepsy, I was unsure. It became suddenly apparent that he suffered from some problem when the car began swerving back and forth along the road after departing the airport. My concern turned to alarm when I noticed the motion of his head sloping downward and snapping erect—he was falling asleep at the wheel.

"Wake up!" I shouted. "Stop the car!"

After convincing him to pull over to the shoulder of the expressway, I was mortified when his head again lolled forward. He was out like a light.

Upon briefly considering the situation, I stepped from the back of the cab, opened the driver's door and pushed him aside to the front passenger's seat. I adjusted the rearview mirror, snapped my seatbelt, turned on the ignition, and drove *myself* home.

When I reached the house, the driver was still asleep. I parked the taxi, turned off the lights, and locked the doors, leaving him to his own siesta while I hurried through the front door to enjoy my own.

He received no tip.

In my entire life, I have never questioned why I consistently find myself in these interesting situations. I just do what is necessary.

Despite my increasingly demanding travel schedule, I found myself employing a variety of innovative techniques to balance business and family. I learned as I went and applied them to my daily activities at work and home.

The one thing with which we are all born equal is twenty-four hours in the day. I discovered that it is how we use those twenty-four hours that separate us. Time cannot be managed. We cannot slow it down. We cannot speed it up. I learned to manage myself by making lists, thereby enabling me to keep control of my priorities.

I began organizing my daily paperwork by using a coding system of colored folders—blue for happy projects, green for financial projects, and red for the "icky" things that I did not really wish to deal with. As these things rarely become more pleasant when postponed, the color red reminded me to finish them as soon as possible and get them over with.

At some point, I read that the most successful people awaken several hours before anyone else and I began doing the same. Arising at 5:00 a.m. gave me an extra hour each day and by the end of the week, those hours afforded me an extra work day.

It was not easy. There were many nights that I returned to the office and worked into the early morning hours just to catch up on the growing piles of paperwork.

Meanwhile, as business grew, so did the headaches. There were days when what I wanted more than anything else in the world was to collapse, hide in the safety of my own home, and cry.

Despite the growth, meeting the payroll was often a problem, especially when large customers like department stores did not pay their bills on time.

Success sometimes breeds intense envy and with it the strong desire among others to covet the same success, despite the fact that they have not worked for it.

Preparing and planning

One day, I received a telephone call from a Jovan representative who rudely demanded an appointment, adding: "It would be in your best interest to have legal representation present."

"Why is a lawyer necessary?" I asked.

"Because what we wish to discuss with you is a legal matter," I was told.

Confused, I called my favorite legal advisor, Lee Miglin, and the following Friday morning three lawyers representing Jovan descended upon my office. Not once did any of these men look directly at me. Instead, they addressed Lee, making a concerted effort to speak over and around me as if I were not even present. They informed him of their intention to challenge the registration of the name Pheromone in federal court.

It was that simple. They wished to have the name and saw no need to ask. They would, instead, just take it.

I was stunned. "Can they do this?" I asked Lee. "I own the name!"

I was mortified when Jovan's attorney's then produced a series of mock-up drawings detailing *their* own product line using *my* registered name of Pheromone.

I thought I had followed the rules of business, doing everything in the most professional manner. I crossed each "t" and dotted every "i," paying careful attention to every detail. And yet, there I sat with these men from a huge company with unlimited financial resources, who had walked into my own office and smugly threatened to destroy it. Their condescending manner and blatant threats infuriated me.

"They cannot do this!" I exclaimed, turning to Lee. He was equally incredulous.

"I own that name!" I repeated.

Unfortunately, in our increasingly litigious society, it is possible to bring legal action against anyone for any reason, often leaving innocent parties no choice but to exhaust all possible personal and financial avenues in order to defend themselves. Jovan wrongly assumed that they could frighten me into submission with their threat of an expensive court battle.

They were very much mistaken.

To me, there was no alternative but to defend my name, and I scraped together a quarter-of-a-million dollars in order to do so. It cost an extraordinarily substantial sum of money to contest their suit—an amount which reduced me to worrying, once again, how I would meet my bills and the payroll.

As litigation pressed on, Jovan was eventually sold to Unilever. Lee arranged a meeting to discuss an out-of-court settlement and it was finally agreed that Unilever could use the word "pheromone," but only in lower case letters and not as the name of their fragrance.

I have never believed that greed propels anyone toward success. Those who are mean, spiteful, and unprofessional, with no regard for others, find their actions returned to them on other levels. Jovan's fragrance was not a success and is no longer on the market today.

Life never ceased to amaze me.

The downside of running a profitable business was not only a matter of lawsuits. Much of the time, it seemed that the frustrations increasingly outweighed the rewards of being an entrepreneur.

One day, dozens of my beautiful Pheromone crystal perfume bottles, nestled in exquisite jewel boxes and ready for shipment, were destroyed. The shelf upon which they were being stored collapsed, shattering every single one of them. It was a fifty-thousand dollar loss.

Around that same time, I was also becoming perplexed over substantial losses in inventory. I could not imagine what could be happening to my product. Out of sheer frustration one evening, I walked alone into a tavern on the opposite side of the street from my warehouse. I asked the bartender and several other regular customers if they had noticed anything unusual transpiring at my building.

"Lady, you've got problems!" one of them said. "Every night a truck pulls up to the loading dock and they pack up boxes of your stuff."

Later, I was able to pinpoint the blame on my warehouse supervisor and took appropriate action.

I was devastated.

Increasingly, I was unable to keep track of each detail of my company. Given my travel schedule and the list of growing commitments, it became necessary for me to explore the possibility of finding someone to help me manage the growth and day-to-day operations. I was only one woman. Each time I attempted to secure an effective general manager for my company, however, I was met with renewed frustration.

With each senior manager, the situation became worse instead of better. One high-level consultant took it upon himself to make financial decisions which affected the entire company, without first discussing it with Lee or me. Under his management, and without our knowledge, my accounts payable department initiated drastic changes, including the restructuring of my employee's payroll schedule.

As times changed, it was also necessary for me to keep the company and our technology up to speed. My initial computer system was an unqualified nightmare from the moment it was installed.

Following the recommendation of several colleagues, I hired a man to install a new electronic management system. Each day, he told me, "Ten more minutes, Mrs. Miglin, just ten more minutes."

Ten more minutes became "Just one more day, Mrs. Miglin." That lead to "one more month," and inevitably, "just a few more months." A year later, the system was still not working properly, causing more problems than before its installation.

The salon in the 1980s

I arrived at my office one morning to find this man sprawled over his computer, sound asleep. After investing more money than I could possibly begin to justify, I asked that he not return. As a result, I was forced to begin the project all over again. To make matters worse, I later discovered that the software he was attempting to work with had been specifically designed for a

175

stand-alone manufacturing company, rather than encompassing both retail and wholesale.

When I first opened the salon, the sales history of every single customer was transcribed by hand on index cards maintained by Helen and me. At one point, we stored over sixty-five thousand names and managed the inventory more effectively than any computer. Today, I hold a fond place in my heart for the days in which the very sight of a computer monitor did not lead me to an anxiety attack.

I had been hindered by lawsuits, was frustrated by a lack of capital, and sick to my stomach over a number of situations. Every time I thought I was back on track, I found myself attacking a new problem. Each disappointment was followed by inevitable frustration.

Many times, I wondered if I should consider selling my business and moving on. Given my success, there were plenty of offers. Since I had established such a well-known and respected brand, it was as easy as taking the money and walking away. At one particularly low point when I finally reached a level of unsated anxiety, I decided to further explore the possibility of doing so.

Traveling to New York, I made an appointment with an investment firm that had previously indicated an interest in acquiring my company. These gentlemen were pleased to meet with me, but our conversation was stopped cold when I was told that when the deal had closed, my presence and advice were not wanted.

"But, I'm the one who built the business," I explained. "How can you run the company without my consultation? I'm the one who understands the customers and the brand!

I was told, quite matter-of-factly, that my future participation would not be necessary. Needless to say, I returned to Chicago rather humbled. It took that particular event to bring me back to reality. It was no more possible for me to sell the business I had worked so passionately to establish than it would be sell my soul.

I continued to do the best I could, safely harboring the knowledge sustained from each collective experience. The low points were inevitably followed by moments of great excitement and adventure.

Despite the long, hard hours that Lee and I invested in both our respective business and responsibilities, family remained our highest priority.

We continued to make it a point in including Duke and Marlena in everything we did and whenever possible, wherever our increased travel schedule took us. At every opportunity, we used those trips as a means of creating exciting and memorable family adventures, and what adventures they were.

The family vacationing together in Palm Springs

177

CHAPTER SEVEN

Now that you hold Destiny in your hands, the future is yours. Change one moment and nothing is ever the same.

riving east along the shore of Lake Geneva, Switzerland—past gingerbread cities and secret gateways of the rich and famous known as the Swiss Riviera—Lee and I traveled through the city of Rolle, where Marlena and Duke were attending the famed Le Rosey summer camp.

There, for six weeks, they studied language, shared cultures, and experienced a camaraderie we hoped would influence and shape the rest of their lives. It was the second year they had done so. Duke was twelve and Marlena was fifteen going on twenty.

While we thought it would be wonderful to have the children spend summers studying in Europe, we never left them alone anywhere, especially halfway around the world from our home. Thus, we devised plans to always vacation nearby while they tested their wings in a world of their own, without actually *being* alone.

That year, the plan called for Lee and me to spend the first two weeks of July at a wonderful hotel in Gstaad, only a few hours away from the children. During the week, he and I toured and dined our way throughout the region. On weekends, we collected Marlena and Duke from school, heading deep into the Alps for family outings.

At the end of two weeks, Helen came to Gstaad to look after the children, while Lee and I returned briefly to the U.S. to catch up on our businesses. We then flew back to Switzerland for the final two weeks of vacation and to accompany Marlena and Duke back home in mid-August, when summer camp ended.

And so it had been for two wonderful summers.

Now, driving again toward Gstaad for the second of our two weeks, I marveled aloud at the stunning scenery.

It was a beautiful Saturday morning. With both hands firmly upon the wheel, he followed close behind the white van in front of us, dispatched to lead us deep into the Alps on a much-anticipated Miglin family adventure.

The six week Le Rosey summer camp season was now over and we had collected the children from school the previous evening, before spending our last weekend in Switzerland. Together, we sought a particularly memorable way to wrap up our vacation.

On that particular day, "up" would certainly prove to be operative word.

Turning to look over my shoulder at Marlena and Duke nestled in the back seat, I became momentarily lost in thought. How much they had matured during that summer in Europe.

Throughout their childhood, whenever we were apart, we always kept in constant communication. There were lots of loving phone calls and a steady stream of both letters and postcards flowing both ways, all with the same Miglin family code. Each of them began with "Dear M and D," and ended with "love, M and D." Mom and Dad, Marlena and Duke—it worked either way. And so it had been from the time they learned to read and write.

We had always been a wonderfully close family and that particular day, climbing thirty-six hundred feet above sea level into the Alps, I felt particularly proud and blessed.

Our destination was the *Balloon-Hafen* of Gstaad, which translated into "Balloon Haven," as in hot air balloon.

Lee parked the car and a barrel-chested man emerged from a nearby building. His name was Captain Hans Bruker, our host for the day. When he thrust his huge hand toward Lee and bellowed, "Velcome, Mishter Meeglin," I sighed with relief, despite the fact that he had an extremely limited English repertoire.

Hans explained that it would take about thirty minutes to unload and inflate the hot air balloon and then we would take a two-hour ride high into the Alpine valley. Checking his watch, he offered for us to wait inside, but we declined.

Instead, as Captain Hans helped his crew unload the balloon from the van we had followed, we listened to Duke read aloud, excitedly, from the brochures Lee and I had been given earlier at the hotel.

"Hot air ballooning is one of the last real adventures," he recited. "It says that the balloon we're going up in has eighty-eight thousand cubic feet of lifting power and is designed to carry up to six people with tanks and equipment.

"The rattan wicker basket is made from a special ground ivy that only grows in Borneo," he continued. "It is particularly good at absorbing the shock of occasional rough landings."

"That's reassuring," Marlena deadpanned.

Duke looked up from the brochure.

"Hey," he added, "insurance is included."

"Oh my, how lovely," I gulped, glancing questioningly at Lee, who was obviously as excited as the children.

When the pear-shaped balloon was filled to capacity, Captain Hans tipped the basket up, checked his watch and called, "You come."

Upon closer inspection, I was pleasantly relieved to find that Borneo's finest wicker was actually a sturdy cockpit. Stepping gingerly inside the gondola, we found a brilliant cathedral of light pouring through the thin dacron and nylon panels, creating a breathtaking stained-glass effect.

Reaching above his head, Captain Hans used a small igniter to fire up the burners and then—much like a train engineer—he gave one swift, hard pull on the hand-operated throttle. I was not prepared for the incredibly loud *whoosh* that accompanied the four feet of flame that, in repeated bursts, began to slowly lift the balloon upright.

The crew below waved as our pilot gave one long pull on the blast valve and we felt the sensation of rising much more quickly, not unlike being in an elevator.

"Bon Voyage!" they called out. "We'll be there to pick you up when you land."

As we continued our ascension, visual relationships began to change. The meadow beneath us grew smaller and sheer cliffs gave way to a steep drop hundreds of feet down into a rugged valley below. We caught our first crosswind and began quickly drifting northeast, over the foreboding depths of the cold and dark, deepening valley.

We were on our way, and *loving* every moment.

For the first fifteen or twenty minutes, we rose very little, lazily drifting along the rim of the valley, two or three hundred feet below. The white van below sped along the highway, generally headed in the same direction.

Over a meadow filled with cows, I was struck by the total silence, and how clearly one could hear the gentle wind and occasional cowbell. Pointing to the cattle below, Captain Hans grinned and gave the throttle a pull, setting forth another loud whoosh of flame. The startled cows below scattered in all directions. Duke and Marlena laughed, and we began climbing higher.

Passing over Gstaad, we commented upon the countless fields of beautiful, fragrant white flowers, which seemed to grow everywhere. Duke thought they looked like patches of snow, which they did. It was truly awe-inspiring and one of the most beautiful sights I have ever experienced.

Floating high above that elegant sea of peace and serenity, I felt calm and centered. It was as if I were discovering a kind of unplanned destiny

For the next hour, we drifted from point to point, rising continually higher and higher in the updrafts created by the early afternoon sun heating the mountain faces around us. Whenever our balloon's heated air began to cool, Captain Hans added a blast or two of flame to maintain our cruising altitude.

We were now so high, so far out over the ever-deepening valley, that the white van below was no longer in visible—nor was the roadway. In fact, civilization was no longer in sight either. As the air became cooler, a sudden cross wind carried us even higher, sweeping us around the end of an enormous range of mountains towering thousands of feet above.

We sailed far above the clouds and Duke and Marlena pointed to our shadow dancing across their tops.

"Very rare," noted Captain Hans. "Almost never."

Earlier that week, while enjoying one of our day excursions, Lee and I had come across a large international glider convention, where enthusiasts the from world over had gathered to fly their crafts in the strong Alpine wind currents.

In addition to being one heck of a good salesman, Lee had also served as a pilot in the service and it took him only minutes to convince two pilots to take us up for a ride. Before I had time to think it over, we were ensconced in two different gliders, each with an experienced pilot. Towed aloft by small single-engine planes, when we reached the proper altitude, we were quite simply, cut loose.

For the next thirty minutes, we soared skyward, lifted by thermals and swept along by the wind, like birds in flight. Through the bubble of my glider, I smiled and gave the thumbs up signal to Lee as he and his pilot entered a steeply banked turn only fifty feet away. My pilot dove in behind them as well.

The swoops, the swirls, and the rise were truly exhilarating, but nothing like the simple peace and total serenity of careening high above the mountains in our hot air balloon.

Suddenly, the gentle breeze was replaced by a more forceful cross current, swerving us directly toward the face of a mountain. Captain Hans pulled the throttle, sending us quickly upward, and reached for his walkie talkie. We had been aloft for well over two and a half hours, and he knew it was time to think about ending our flight.

But where? We were at the mercy of the wind.

All around us were sheer cliffs and steep rock faces filled with snow. Far below, the valley floor lie buried in cool blue shadows. Speaking calmly into his radio, Captain Hans received only static in return and smiled at us. Nervously, we returned his smile.

After numerous attempts at contact, to which Hans received only garbled words in response—some of which sounded like "Ve can't zxzxzxzx you . . . where xzxzxzxzx you?" he turned and delivered somewhat chilling news.

"We a little lost," he admitted.

We began wondering just how serious our situation was.

Passing over a jagged ridge, we saw a small green meadow drenched in rolling beds of flowering white Edelweiss. Toward one end, stood a weathered farmhouse and shed with its barn-type doors wide open.

With great authority, Captain Hans announced, "We land now. Brace yourself for crash!"

My heart began to race. It seemed the balloon was swooping in rather fast, driven by the crosswinds and the balloon's air, which the Captain did not reheat. We were about fifteen feet above the ground when a large dog began running in circles below, barking noisily.

At ten feet, our grip on the rail tightened. We looked to Captain Hans for reassurance. He smiled and nodded. We smiled back, although the *Titanic* came to mind.

When we were sailing only five feet above the ground, a man and woman came running out of the farm house.

There was a swishing sound as the bottom edge of the basket made first contact with blades of grass. Then, as Captain Hans barked, "Now!" He pulled an emergency release cord that opened up the balloon, allowing the air to quickly escape and prevent us from being dragged along the ground. Lee and I held on tightly to Duke and Marlena.

All at once, we were on our side. Then rolling into a sea of yellow, orange and fiery red nylon, we lost sight of the farmhouse, then the ground, then each other.

It was over in a split second, and for a moment there was dead silence.

Then, I heard Duke laughing and saw his head pop up out of the fabric, his face being licked by an overly friendly Golden Retriever. Next, up popped Marlena, and then Lee.

"We all okay?" called Captain Hans, climbing to his feet and brushing himself off.

"Yes! Danke!" we shouted.

I was so grateful that we had landed unharmed. What could have been a serious situation was instead another Miglin moment, filled with adventure and fun.

Turning to the farmer and his wife who had run to the balloon to ascertain our safety, Hans launched into a rapid stream of Swiss German, of which I could only pick up an occasional word or two.

As neither the farmer nor his wife spoke any English, she simply motioned with her hand for us to follow. We brushed ourselves off and headed for the farmhouse. Her husband remained behind with Captain Hans, who returned to his efforts of trying to communicate with his crew on the walkie talkie.

The house was in a remote area. There was no telephone and it was apparent that we would be there for quite some time.

The farmer and his wife were gracious hosts. As the sun began to set, the temperature of the high mountain air dropped quickly. They lit a warming fire and offered us homemade bread, soup, cheese, and a wonderful coffee which warmed the soul.

The farmer's wife, we discovered, spoke a little French, and we were able to communicate somewhat. Outside in his shed, her husband proudly displayed to us fifteen enormous wheels of cheese he was in the process of aging.

Just then, we heard the sound of an automobile. I was quite relieved to see Hans' crew waving wildly from the window of the van as it approached.

"Allo!" they shouted. "We found you!"

Somehow, they had managed to decode Hans' garbled SOS. Before climbing into the van for the long ride back, we thanked our hosts warmly. Then, while the men rolled up the balloon and loaded the basket, Marlena and I walked over to a nearby field of brilliant white flowers.

Lit only by pale moonlight, they seemed to glow in the dark of the night. Their petals were soft and buttery and the white leaves felt warm and fuzzy in spite of the cool night air. Carefully picking two or three sprigs, I closed my eyes and held them close to my nose, drinking in the fresh purity of their scent.

It was a moment I wished to lock in my memory forever.

For months after returning from Switzerland, the vision of white flowers cascading over the meadows kept appearing in my mind. Whenever it did, a comforting sense of inner-peace and spirituality swept over my entire being.

For many years I had been interested in Eastern cultures, researching the Seven Sacred Chakras found in Buddhist and Hindu scriptures. I found those deeply spiritual messages to be both inspirational and quietly powerful. How beautiful it would be, I thought, to draw from those ancient teachings by utilizing only pure white flowers associated with different chakra points in the body to evoke a certain response.

In the months that followed, I worked many long days, often well into the night, researching the purest and most ethereal flowers in the world. With Vito Lenoci, I began isolating and combining delicate essential oils of the world's most exquisite white flowers, each of which carried messages, centuries old, to arouse the senses and inspire the soul.

From the middle east, we imported the sacred Kyphi, also known as the graceful calla lily, to lend strength and dignity. We chose Tekh, the romantic white rose from Bulgaria, to open the heart to give and receive unconditional love.

Months later, I discovered the intricate powers of Osmanthus, a delicate flower gathered from the highest Himalyan peaks, where Tibetan monks believe their immortal souls touch the hand of God.

Soon after, I added three more white blooms with revitalizing qualities to nurture a woman's most intimate being. Narcissus, namesake of Greek mythology, and known as the flower of inner-vision, helps a woman find her center. The exotic white orchid recharges the intuitive mind with new energy, while potent Karo-Karunde, which grows wild on the volcanic soil of southern Africa, contains a scent that can be detected more than a mile away.

And from the Orient, I imported the oils of the sensual Fo-Ti-Tieng, revered by the last Emperor of China as a sexual stimulant.

When finished, what I originally thought might only take months had actually taken over four years to create. I knew, however, that my new fragrance would help a woman achieve an aura of calm and confidence and help inspire her to achieve her greatest ambitions.

And so it was, that my beautiful fragrance Destiny was born.

Sharing it with the rest of the world, however, became yet another challenge. It seemed that my entire company was against taking it to market and to make matters worse, I received tremendous resistance from my sales representatives in the department store field.

"It's too ethereal," they complained. "We'll never be able to sell it."

To make matters worse, they also expressed great hesitation over the manner in which I wished to position it. It was time to address both the sensuality and spirituality of women, but no other fragrance company had dared to make such a bold statement with their marketing.

Why, I wondered, was life so filled with challenges! I knew in my heart and with my entire being that it was a fragrance that would make history.

I initiated the most ingenious marketing plan the fragrance industry had ever seen. Rather than launching yet another perfume using traditional advertising and in-store modeling, I decided to do something that would benefit all women. I would create a reason for women to wear my fragrance and to gain new, positive energy from the experience of doing so.

Reflecting upon all that I had learned from networking with other successful women, I drafted a list of more than two-hundred friends and associates accomplished in their own chosen fields. When I finished, the list included women in business, the arts, education and other professions, including government, fashion, finance, law, interior design, advertising, architecture, publishing, real estate, science, health care, fitness and travel.

These were women of vision who had transformed their dreams into reality. They had achieved an integration of inner conviction and commitment in every dimension of their lives.

It became *my* vision to tap into their energy and knowledge and share it with others. How wonderful it would be, I thought, to foster one-on-one guidance from these professionals to young hopefuls. For years, men had been networking with great success, while women were left with a somewhat "underground" approach in embracing these same principals. I wished to establish an opportunity for young women to benefit from formal guidance, very much like that which was a part of the male corporate culture.

When I explained my idea to everyone on my list, their response was both enthusiastic and affirmative. Each of them agreed to serve as a mentor for others just starting out in their professional careers. Thus, this impressive group of powerhouse talent became "Women of Destiny."

Intertwining this mentoring program with the launch of my newest perfume at Marshall Field's, one-hundred sixty-eight of my two-hundred mentors gathered for an elegant cocktail reception to kick off the Women of Destiny program. Open to women eighteen and older who desired personal guidance in a specific area of interest, applications were available at all Destiny counters in every Marshall Field's store.

Each applicant was invited to submit a one-hundred word letter indicating her goals and reasons for requesting a certain mentor. Beautiful directories profiling each "Woman of Destiny" were also available.

I expected my mentoring program to be a success, but I was not prepared for the overwhelming response. Marshall Field's sales associates were besieged with young women who expressed their desire to succeed in their chosen professions. During the first week of the program, over eighteen-hundred women submitted applications.

Carefully screening each applicant, my committee and I then paired them with mentors who agreed to devote at least eight to ten hours personally working with their proteges in the ensuing months.

In fact, Women of Destiny was such a rousing triumph that a group of the original mentors formed the Destiny Institute in order to continue the program with a new group of young women. It became a bridge between aspiration and experience, reaffirming my vision of assisting women in recognizing their own power to shape their futures.

While it was one thing to inspire and guide young women, there was another social tragedy crying out for attention.

Over the course of several years, I had been forced to say good-bye in life to many special friends who were dying from AIDS. I did everything possible to increase public awareness of this terrible pandemic, and when Marshall Field's asked for my participation in a fund-raising event to benefit the AIDS Foundation, I did not hesitate.

That evening, Marshall Field's executives shared with me their delight over the Women of Destiny program. "It's been so successful," they said enthusiastically, "we'd like you to create another phenomenal promotion for us."

At the Visions of Destiny's art show

It dawned on me that evening that I could use Destiny to further the fight against AIDS.

I personally selected twenty-five outstanding young contemporary artists and requested that they create their own interpretation of destiny through paintings, sculpture, photography, textiles and mixed media installations. These stunning pieces of art were then displayed at Marshall Field's as "Visions of Destiny," and later auctioned at an elegant gala to benefit the Chicago House, a not-for-profit organization providing housing and social services for men and women living with AIDS.

The increased awareness it lent to the thousands of people in our city fighting for their lives against AIDS was a tremendous success. Women of Destiny and Visions of Destiny remain two of my proudest achievements.

When we reach out to others, embracing our own particular talents, we can change the lives of others. It takes but one person to make a difference.

CHAPTER EIGHT

estiny was a success, Pheromone was recognized as a classic, and my business was acknowledged as one of the top-ten woman owned companies in Chicago.

One afternoon, I received a telephone call from Irv Kupcinet, Chicago's legendary celebrity journalist. Many years ago, it was "Kup," as he was affectionately known, who helped give me a jump-start with a mention in his daily column. An endorsement from Kup was as good as gold and over the years, he and his wife Essee, a longtime customer, became wonderful supporters.

"What are you and Lee doing on Friday, April 23?" asked Kup.

"I don't know that we have any definitive plans," I answered, unable to determine the direction of the conversation.

"Great!" he said. "Mark your calendar, Marilyn. The Variety Club would like to honor you and Lee as King and Queen of Hearts at an award dinner tribute."

After collecting my thoughts, I picked up the phone and called Lee at his office. "Darling," I purred, "How would you like to honored by the Variety Club as Chicago's King of Hearts?"

I held my breath waiting for his response. Lee was a private man who derived joy from my own recognition by the media. He was shy, however, about any public acknowledgment of his own civic and business efforts, preferring instead to remain out of the limelight.

Much to my relief, he said, "Why, that's a wonderful honor. I would be proud to accept it."

And so it was that we were recognized at a gala benefit which included a moving video tribute of our mutual contributions to the City of Chicago. It was a sparkling, memorable evening, and we were genuinely touched.

Shortly thereafter, we decided to reward ourselves for our hard work with a trip to Europe. Usually, Marlena and Duke accompanied us on such vacations, but this time would be different. It would be just the two of us. We looked forward to our time together and planned a romantic trip, revisiting many of the quaint hotels and locales we had previously enjoyed with the children.

For several glorious days, we wined and dined ourselves at the Palace Hotel in Gstaad. On the final evening of our stay in Switzerland, the hotel's owner, Ernst, joined us for dinner and we enjoyed an animated conversation, reliving past adventures. When we discussed our plans to take the train to Rome the next morning, Ernst's jovial tone turned to one of somber concern.

"Ah," he said, frowning. "You must be very careful there. Motorcyclists in Italy are snatching handbags and jewelry from unsuspecting tourists and then driving off. Take precautions."

As a safeguard, Ernst advised us to pack all of our valuables into one suitcase. Heeding his warning, we did just that, carefully organizing all of our belongings. The only two items that I

My family with Kup at the Variety Club Award dinner

Lee thanking the Variety Club for the honor they bestowed on us

did not pack were my watch and my beautiful diamond engagement ring. Everything else, including my pearls and the rest of
my jewelry went into one suitcase, per Ernst's instructions.

The next morning, we drove to Geneva, where we boarded
the train and enjoyed a romantic ride through the mountains.
Upon reaching the border, there was some sort of commotion.
As neither Lee nor I spoke Italian, we paid little attention to the
announcements being made. Little did we know that our luggage was removed from the train for a customs' check.

We arrived at the station in Rome and de-trained. Our luggage, however, was nowhere to be found. "Not to worry," we were
assured. Our bags would most certainly be on the next train from
Geneva.

As our suitcases contained *all* of our personal belongings, I
was not exactly thrilled at the prospect of spending our first
day in Rome without being afforded the luxury of a change of
clothes. There was little if nothing that we could do and so we
made our way to our hotel. There, we were met with stares of
curiosity upon checking in without luggage.

While Lee instigated a conversation with the hotel concierge,
asking him to check on our luggage, an interesting-looking
gentleman overhead their topic of discussion and made his way
over to them. He introduced himself as Roberto, and expressed
his concern over our lost belongings.

"Is there anywhere you plan on visiting tomorrow?" he inquired, adding that he happened to be a "driver."

"Well," answered Lee, "I'm not sure. We hope to find our
luggage before even thinking about anything else."

We freshened up to the best of our ability and set out to
purchase a few new pieces of clothing and toiletries. The fact
that all the stores in Rome were closed that day did nothing but
add to our frustration.

Finally, the next train from Geneva arrived on schedule. Our
suitcases, however, were not aboard.

That evening, I carefully washed out the white blouse I had been wearing since our departure from Gstaad. The next morning, we took a car to the Swiss-Italian border, where officials from both countries pointed blame toward the other.

The Swiss insisted that the Italians had confiscated our baggage, while the Italians remained indignant, suggesting that our belongings were being held by the Swiss.

Our things were never to be seen again.

Back at the hotel, Lee resumed his pleas with the concierge for assistance in retrieving our luggage. As fate would have it, Roberto, the kind Italian we had met the previous afternoon, was sitting in the lobby. Once again, he overhead Lee's conversation and in short order approached us.

"Please," he implored. "It is not right that you're so sad in my country. I would like to help you," he implored.

Our arrival in Rome had been the only glitch in an otherwise wonderful vacation. Luggage or no luggage, we decided to make the best of our situation and engaged Roberto's expertise in driving us on a sight-seeing tour. Little did we know upon doing so that we were about to enjoy spectacular scenery and sights rarely enjoyed by most Romans.

The following day, at the appointed time, Roberto was waiting for us in the hotel lobby. His enthusiasm was infectious. "Okay! Where you like to see first?" he exclaimed, clapping his hands.

Lee and I had a long list of sights we wished to visit and did not know where to begin.

"Well," I offered, "I would like to see the Sistine Chapel and the Vatican."

Roberto turned around in the driver's seat and asked me, "Is the Signora Catholic?"

I nodded.

"Ah! This is good. Is the Signora Polish, by chance?"

Again, I nodded, looking at Lee, who merely shrugged.

"Ah-ha!" said Roberto. "This is very, very good!" With that, he started the engine and off we drove to St. Peter's Square.

Without having seen the Sistine Chapel, one cannot form an appreciation of what man is capable of achieving. An otherwise unremarkable structure with a plain brick façade, it was originally designed to serve as the pope's private ceremonial chapel. The Vatican, next door, became the permanent papal residence and today the Sistine Chapel is used by the College of Cardinals when in session to elect a new pope.

As Roberto escorted us inside, I was not prepared for the visions of such awe-inspiring grandeur, which took my breath away. In 1481, Pope Sistus IV summoned to Rome Florentine painters to decorate the walls of the chapel with spectacular frescoes. The vaulted ceiling was painted in blue with a star-spangled sky. Twenty-five years later, Pope Julius II commissioned Michelangelo to repaint the ceiling, adorning it with such enlightenment and perfection in detail that it was sufficient to illuminate a world which for so many hundreds of years had remained in a state of darkness.

Working high above the chapel floor, lying on his back on scaffolding, Michelangelo created some of the finest images of all time. He included nine scenes from the book of Genesis, beginning with God Separating Light from Darkness and including the Creation of Adam, the Creation of Eve, the Temptation, the Fall of Adam and Eve, and the Flood.

As Roberto described to us in detail the rich history of each panel and the surrounding frescoes, Lee and I were mesmerized. Never before had I seen such beauty. He also provided a brief explanation of the controversial efforts, then underway, to restore the artwork. We were fascinated.

As we listened to Roberto's impressive knowledge of the Sistine Chapel's history, I could not help but sense his irritation over the growing number of visitors and the level of noise inside. During the brief time since we had entered, the crowd of tourists had multiplied to standing room only.

Straightening his posture, Roberto snapped his fingers and pointed to a Monsignor at the opposite end of the room near the altar. Roberto gestured to us and mouthed something to the Monsignor, who made a brief announcement in Italian. To our amazement, the entire crowd parted and began to disperse. As Roberto escorted Lee and me to the altar and introduced us to the Monsignor, I could not imagine what was happening.

To our shock, the Monsignor then manipulated a piece of the wooden altar, initiating a mechanism that opened a wall behind him. Gently patting Lee's shoulder, Roberto urged us through the entry way and escorted us up a staircase. Behind us, the wall swung shut. Atop the stairs, he opened a door which revealed a private residence filled with exquisitely ornate pieces of furniture, jewels, and art. It took a few moments for me to comprehend exactly where I was standing. When the realization finally hit me, I was completely dumbstruck.

We had been escorted into the Pope's private apartment!

I felt dizzy.

"Who *are* you?" I blurted to Roberto. He turned slowly to face us and humbly bowed.

"Ah, Signora," he said, his eyes shining. "I am the driver of the former Pope. My sons now drive the new Pope, John Paul."

To say that we were shocked would be an understatement. As Lee and I listened to this man detail his history of service to the Pope and the unbridled love, affection and respect he held for him, I felt as though I were having an out of body experience. Looking about the room at the Pope's vestments, I could hardly breathe.

Roberto walked over to an ornate display case and withdrew a ring. "This is my favorite Pope's ring," he announced approaching me, ring in hand. "It belonged to Pope John. Would the Signora like to try it on?"

Unable to speak, I managed only a stiff nod.

Memories exploded of the former Pope's visit to Chicago. Although he was an Archbishop at that time, he had presided over my childhood confirmation and I had bowed to kiss his ring.

I realized as Roberto slipped it onto my finger, that this was the very ring I had kissed so many years ago. How proud my grandmother would have been! The only other thought I could focus upon was the size of the ring itself. The Pope had indeed been a substantial man.

As Lee and I attempted to collect ourselves, Roberto stepped to a window overlooking a garden. He clapped his hands together and rubbed them excitedly. "Ah!" he exclaimed. "This is good! His Eminence is in the garden. I take you outside to meet him. Come! Come!"

I could not move my feet. Lee had to nudge me forward to follow Roberto, who explained that the Pope was very stressed about a forthcoming trip to Poland and that he would keep the introduction brief.

I was so nervous that I could barely say hello in English, let alone Polish. The motion made in kneeling to kiss his ring was as if I were operating in slow-motion. Everything around me seemed to stop. He graciously spent a few moments with us before Roberto escorted us away.

"Did the Signora enjoy her tour?" he asked with a smile.

There were, of course, no possible words to express to him our appreciation. He invited us to meet him again the following day for a tour of Vatican City. Needless to say, we excitedly accepted his offer and thanked him again for his kindness before bidding him good-bye.

We returned to our hotel completely dazed. The rest of that day, every time I came to from being lost in my own thoughts, I turned to look at Lee. His slack-jawed expression confirmed his shared level of disbelief. We finally had the opportunity that afternoon to purchase new clothes, then enjoyed a quiet dinner before retiring early—but I couldn't sleep. I could not help but wonder what our next visit with Roberto would bring.

The following morning, we dressed and had breakfast in our room overlooking Rome before meeting Roberto and setting forth for Vatican City. This time, when we reached St. Peter's Square and approached the Swiss guards, I felt my chest tightening in apprehension. Roberto merely waved his hand and we were ushered inside.

Remembering my fascination with the stunning frescoes inside the Sistine Chapel, Roberto had arranged for us a special introduction to Professor Cassio, the man responsible for its restoration. He invited us to join him for lunch in a dining room adjacent to his office. At that time, the professor was also the art director for the Vatican. He regaled us with more of the history of the Sistine Chapel's artwork, detailing the progress of the restoration of Michelangelo's panels.

During our discussion the dining room and hallways were a plethora of activity. Nuns rushed in and out, having crosses blessed, and Monsignors busied themselves moving spectacular paintings. We enjoyed our lunch, but could not take our eyes off all of the art surrounding us.

As Professor Cassio continued sharing with us the background of many of the pieces which caught our eye, the conversation fell silent when Lee asked, "Is any of this artwork for sale?"

Roberto's eyes widened in delight.

"Call the Pope," he urged a Monsignor. "Ask him if we cannot sell something to these nice people."

Nodding, the Monsignor lifted the receiver of a red phone. Again, my stomach fluttered upon realizing that it was a direct line to the Pope himself. As the Monsignor initiated an animated conversation in Italian, I locked eyes with Lee in silence, hold-

With one of our Vatican masterpieces

ing my breath. Roberto listened closely to the Monsignor's conversation, smiling warmly at us.

Finally, the Monsignor nodded to Roberto, "Yes," and returned the phone to its cradle.

"What would you like to purchase?" asked Roberto.

We could not believe that this was really happening. We looked about and saw a beautiful gold-gilded frame from the twelfth century. We saw stunning paintings, including some which adorned wooden tabletops. It was overwhelming.

Finally, we settled upon twenty-eight pieces, which were eventually shipped to the United States aboard the Vatican plane, incurring no international duty. It was a special miracle we had been blessed with and had we not lost our luggage, we would never have enjoyed such a grand adventure.

Several months later at a New York dinner party, I found myself sitting next to one of the most formidable art dealers in the country. I listened silently, as he regaled fellow guests with stories of his acquisitions, their history, and value. Finally, I could no longer resist.

"Have you ever met anyone who owns a collection of art from the Vatican?" I asked.

"Impossible!" he boomed, shaking his head. "There is no one who has such a collection. The Vatican *does not* sell its art!"

From across the table, Lee smiled.

Marlena finished high school and was accepted at Boston University, where she planned to study journalism. Duke meanwhile was accepted into the Air force Academy, following in his father's footsteps by becoming a pilot. Both of them were growing into fine young adults and as parents, we could not have been more proud.

It seemed odd, at first, when the children were no longer at home. Lee in particular found their absence quite difficult at times and never failed to remind them how much they were loved. Upon her birthday, one year in Boston, Marlena was summoned to the mail room of her dormitory. It seemed that she had received, in one day, more mail than the University officials could comprehend. She was absolutely mortified to discover hundreds of envelopes written in familiar handwriting and with great embarrassment, she explained to the dormitory director, that each envelope had been addressed by her father.

With the assistance of several of Marlena's friends, boxes of envelopes were carried to her dorm room. When at last she was alone, she began to open them one by one. Her embarrassment turned to tears of emotion when she realized that each envelope contained a birthday card and a handwritten note from Lee.

"Let me get this straight," one friend told her. "Your dad shut down the mail room by sending you hundreds of handwritten birthday cards?"

"Yes," Marlena nodded.

"That is so cool. I wish *I* had a dad like that."

Back on Oak Street, when an announcement was made that Bloomingdales was coming to Michigan Avenue, just around the corner, many merchants expressed their fear that the new store would take traffic away from our own shopping boulevard. Many of them voiced their concern, and so I organized a meeting with the property owners and store managers to discuss what we would do to effectively market our street. I felt that with the proper promotion, Oak Street could surpass the increasing up-scale image of Michigan Avenue and become as well-known as Rodeo Drive and Fifth Avenue.

Everyone was quite enthusiastic and supportive at the idea of organizing our own merchants' association, but when it came time to nominate not only the board of directors but a president, the meeting fell silent.

"Marilyn, your children are much older than ours," some-one said.

"You have the passion and the determination to make this work," said another. "You should be president and all of us will support you."

And so it was that I formed the Oak Street Council, initiating efforts to recreate and design the street.

I felt it was important to bring together a team of the best creative talent in Chicago to help us capture our shopping district's unique ambiance and communicate its potential. It was my vision to use the Council as a means of promoting Oak Street as a showcase for the world's finest fashions, the most stylish accessories, and unparalleled service.

I began by recruiting internationally-renowned Chicago architect Stanley Tigerman to develop a master plan and to work with individual store and property owners on upgrading their buildings. He developed a concept of "organized individuality," which allowed each building to retain its own identity, and used a distinctive pattern of trees and street lamps to give the street a more cohesive look.

I raised a half-million dollars for new streetscaping, which included twenty-eight beautiful trees, surrounded by decorative grates lit from below, thirty-eight art deco street lamps, and all new sidewalks in a distinctive charcoal gray color.

Our marketing plan was equally ambitious. We organized an exquisite brochure, held a fashion show under an enormous tent that covered the entire street, and brought national attention to Oak Street.

Today, any other shopping boulevard would be hard-pressed to match the wide range of exclusive stores and services that this street offers—all in one city block, where retailers such as Barney's New York, Prada, Hermes, Pratesi, Kate Spade, BCBG, and St. John all continue to support the Oak Street Council.

Because of Oak Street's success, Mayor Daley invited me to join his special committee on tourism. I also was asked to serve as an officer of the Chicago Convention and Tourism Bureau and was appointed by the Governor of Illinois to the state's Board of Economic Development.

Many times I felt overcommitted, unable to take on another new project. It was at precisely one of those moments that I was approached by Roberta Vanderver, the principal of Ogden Elementary—the school that Duke and Marlena had attended, and where I had once been so active as a parent-volunteer.

"Marilyn, we need your help," she said. "The playground is filled with potholes and broken equipment. It's in dangerous condition and each week, we have three or four accidents, with the children getting sprains and fractures. The Board of Education doesn't have the money to help," she lamented, "and so we need to raise the necessary funds to fix it ourselves. We'd like you to chair the project.

Inwardly, I groaned.

"How much money do you need?" I asked.

"Well," she hesitated, "I'm not really sure."

Rising to my feet, I informed her that I could not become involved in any new project that had no specific direction and suggested that she write a business plan.

"But, I don't know how to write a business plan," said Roberta.

"Then research how to do so or find someone to assist you. When you have a solid plan-of-action, we shall then discuss my involvement."

Wishing her good success, I said good-bye, relieved that I could go about my normal routine. I was sure that I would never hear from her again and that I was off the hook.

One year later, to my great surprise, Roberta reappeared with a business plan, outlining the need for four-hundred-thousand dollars to upgrade the playground's equipment.

This time, I could not turn her away and thereby found myself the chairman of the "Friends of Ogden" School.

As I should have known, the thankless task of raising the necessary funds from the community became a pleasure and I became more and more involved in obtaining funds for Ogden. A good school is the catalyst for growth in any community, and it was not difficult to convince the surrounding businesses of the importance of their support.

The first project we undertook was upgrading the playground with a soft surface. Later we added a running track. Then I raised more funds for a beautiful wrought iron fence to enclose the area.

I felt it important to involve the children themselves in the project, and so they designed pieces of art in their classes, which were then incorporated into each pillar of the fence. When we finished, the grounds and the new fence were one of the most delightful sights in the neighborhood.

I was deeply touched when a "Marilyn Miglin Dream Fund" was established at Ogden to benefit less fortunate students who were otherwise unable to attend field trips, or purchase books and supplies.

It was yet one more project from which I derived a tremendous sense of purpose and satisfaction. To this day, when walking past the playground, the sight of the children playing on their new equipment—laughing, running and occasionally stumbling on the soft surface, never fails to make me smile.

Meanwhile, casual cocktail party conversation centered around Lee's announced plans to erect a one-hundred-twenty-five-story office tower in the heart of Chicago. His ambitious plans for the Miglin-Beitler Sky Needle would top the bid for the world's tallest building.

The proposed structure, designed by architect Cesar Pelli, would soar over the one-hundred-ten-story Sears Tower three blocks away.

As Lee worked out the financing for building his dream, our home became an increasing hub of activity. While entertaining an architect at dinner one evening, Lee momentary excused himself from the dining room to retrieve plans detailing the Sky Needle. In his absence, the architect looked at me from across the table and said, "You must be a perfect woman, Marilyn."

Perplexed by his comment, I asked, "What do you mean?"

"Your husband," he explained, "is the greatest perfectionist I have ever met in my entire life. I must commend you for being his wife. You must be absolutely perfect to be with him! That man investigates and critiques every detail. Lee makes it a point to know the history of a doorknob!" he continued. "Before we build a door for him, we have to do our research. *No one* asks more questions than he does."

It was a lovely compliment to Lee's consummate professionalism and passion for detail.

Several months later, we were invited by the Executive's Club of Chicago to serve as business emissaries on a trip to Moscow. Ten business executives, representing wide-ranging fields were chosen to lead this special envoy—the first of its kind to travel to the Soviet Union following the destruction of the Berlin Wall. Lee was selected for his real estate savvy and I was asked to join the group as the only woman business owner. We were honored to have been included in such a historical opportunity. The trip promised to be made even more special by the fact that Marlena would join us in order to cover the events as a journalism student.

Shortly before our scheduled departure, we ran into world-renowned photographer Victor Skrebneski and Michael Kutza, Director of the Chicago International Film Festival, during dinner. We enjoyed a drink together, and Michael shared with us his excitement over his participation at the Moscow Film Festival the following week.

"My goodness, Michael," I said. "Why, *I'm* going to Moscow next week."

"That's wonderful!" he said enthusiastically. "Then you must come to a special party I am hosting!"

"Of course I shall," I promised before bidding them goodnight.

Our arrival in Moscow, presented many odd juxtapositions. The beautiful hotel where we stayed was certainly not what I had expected, nor was the elegant and brilliantly gilded casino in the middle of the lobby.

Lee escorted Marlena into the casino to teach her the nuances of blackjack. I declined to join them. I opted instead to freshen up after the long flight.

After changing my clothes, I returned to the lobby to find the two of them laughing together, playing blackjack. It seemed strange to me. There I was—in the middle of the Soviet Union—watching my husband and daughter gambling in one of the most ornate casinos I had ever seen.

Retrieving the camera from my purse, I carefully framed this image and shot several photographs of the two of them. Suddenly, two cold-faced young men appeared from nowhere. They took me by both arms and unceremoniously escorted me into another room, closing the door behind them.

I had absolutely no idea what was going on. One of the men jerked my camera away from me and removed the film. Before my eyes, he thoroughly destroyed it, while the other man began shouting at me in Russian, and then in broken English.

"You should be arrested! It is against the law to take photographs in the casino!"

As neither Lee or Marlena could have possibly known of my whereabouts or this latest situation I found myself in, I began to panic. After one hour of further interrogation specifically meant to frighten me, I was finally released.

I did not take any other photographs during the course of our visit to Russia.

As the only businesswoman in our envoy, I was sensitive to the other women in the group who had traveled with their husbands. In order to balance my conflicting roles, I alternated between being a businesswoman one day and riding the tour bus with the spouses the next.

One afternoon aboard the bus, I suddenly remembered Michael Kutza's invitation and asked the driver about the location of the Georgian restaurant where his event was being held. As it turned out, the restaurant was not far from our location.

Although we were scheduled to attend a special cocktail reception at the American Embassy at precisely 5:30 that evening, I wanted very much to see Michael as well. Around 3:30 that afternoon, I said to the ladies on the bus, "How would you like the opportunity to have a unique look at Russia that no one else will ever be able to show you?" They voiced their enthusiasm and I convinced the bus driver to stop at the restaurant.

Michael was delighted to see me and the ladies were beside themselves upon being introduced to handsome, bare-chested Russian male movie stars who flirted shamelessly with their unexpected American guests. We all enjoyed a few cocktails.

It was all fun until someone mentioned the time. I was mortified when my wristwatch revealed that it was after 5 p.m. I knew that if I was the cause of our lateness at the Embassy, that the envoy would have my head for embarrassing them.

I thanked Michael and urged the women back onto the bus, silently praying that we would not be late. Shortly before 6 p.m., we arrived at the Embassy—late and completely against protocol. While the other women tittered, I was soundly scolded.

Later that evening, as I sipped champagne, I noticed a dashing man across the room who kept smiling at me. His cool, James Bondish demeanor was rather interesting and before I knew it, he walked over to introduce himself, confirming my suspicions that he was a CIA agent. As we talked, he began flirting with me and asked if I would care to join him for dinner following the reception.

"Oh, my!" I answered coquettishly. "I would love to, but I have twenty-three people with me—including my husband."

"Fine," he said. "Everyone is invited, including your special husband. Just promise me that I can sit next to you."

My earlier reprimand had been long-since forgotten and as our group was in festive spirit, we joined him for dinner at an elegant restaurant with dark, velvet curtains. Our special agent toasted us and we had the time of our lives, continuing to sample warm Russian vodka until three in the morning.

The following day presented a full itinerary of activity. In addition to visiting the Kremlin, where I was to be among the first American businesswomen to be received, we had also scheduled a visit to a Russian perfumery. This side trip necessitated our early departure from our meeting at the Kremlin. When it came time for us to leave, every single man in the room jumped up to ask for my autograph. As a famous American perfumer, it seems that I was an intriguing commodity. The fact that these Russian businessmen completely ignored the other business men in our party was also rather embarrassing to say the least.

At a State dinner later that evening, I found myself seated next to the Russian Minister of Timber. Knowing just enough Russian to be flirtatious, I enjoyed our limited conversation, assuming that his title meant that he managed Russian forests. I was shocked to discover that this man was of such importance and so powerful, that Gorbechev considered him to be his "right arm." His jurisdiction included not only timber, but every single paper product manufactured in the Soviet Union.

My innocent flirtation with the Minister of Timber grew out of control, when the topic of conversation turned to his private dacha, which he invited me to visit.

"What's a dacha?" I asked and the entire room of men burst into laughter.

It must be said that Lee was always nearby to rescue me at the end of an interesting evening and from the many unusual situations in which I found myself.

Back in Chicago, I continued to promote Pheromone and Destiny, but as the recession took hold, my profits began to diminish while the daily frustrations increased. Lee continued to work towards making his dream of developing the world's tallest building a reality.

As the stock market continued to weaken, so did his hopes for securing the necessary financing.

When Marlena transferred to Northwestern University to finish her degree, Duke took advantage of the military academy's "Stop Out" program, using a year off to reflect upon his career options. With increasing cuts in military budgets, his friends in the Air Force, most of them trained as pilots, found themselves relegated to desk jobs or aircraft maintenance. It was clear to Duke at that time that remaining in the military did not necessarily guarantee the future he had once envisioned. The day before the Academy's appointed deadline for Duke's decision, he sat down with Lee to explain his rationale.

"Dad, you wouldn't want your son to remain in a company that's downsizing, would you?" he asked.

Duke, in uniform

Lee and I supported Duke's decision and were very proud when he was accepted to the University of Southern California. When the Gulf War broke out shortly thereafter, I thanked God that he was no longer in the military and joined him in praying for the safety of his friends who were sent to the Middle East.

Somehow, life had changed drastically from the carefree days of the 1980s. Because of the Gulf War, Lee was forced to temporarily abandon his search for financing the Sky Needle. The real

Marlena

estate market slowed to a halt and corporate takeovers surged—
an unfortunate practice that included department stores as well.
Smaller stores went out of business and the larger chains that
remained were either purchased or consolidated.

As a result, my fragrance sales steadily began to decline.
Maintaining counter space became increasingly difficult as the
recession hit full stride. In the course of one year, I lost fifty

percent of the department store business I had worked so passionately to build.

All around me, the winds of change were howling. It was time to reinvent myself as I had done so often before. How I would do it was not as important as recognizing the fact that I needed to find alternative means to maintain my foothold.

The answer I sought would present itself in short order.

CHAPTER NINE

"Trust yourself. That is the only courage you need to succeed."

$\mathscr{S}$erendipity comes, sometimes, not by chance, but from the energy one projects into the universe.

While visiting New York on business one day, I met with Jules Schlessinger, a long time-friend in the cosmetics industry.

"Marilyn, have you ever seen those shopping programs on television?" he asked excitedly. "I know a woman named Joanne Benjamin, who's doing some special things with the Home Shopping Club. Have you ever thought about selling your products on TV?"

I shook my head.

"Well, I think you'd be a big hit," he said. "You could expose your brand to a wider market than the luxury stores."

I had already determined that it was time to investigate new opportunities, and Jules's enthusiasm was contagious. Every person opens new doors for those courageous enough to step through. It was immediately apparent that Jules was giving me a shove through a new entrance way.

I knew very little about mass sales on television. Nevertheless, I made an appointment with Joanne Benjamin, president of a marketing company called ACI, to discuss the possibility of my making a presentation to the Home Shopping buyers. We met at the Plaza Hotel's Palm Court restaurant, and liked each other immediately. So impressed was she about my beautiful products that the next day she arranged for Sandy Renfrow, at that time Home Shopping's marketing director, to meet with the two of us at Joanne's office.

Excited about this new business opportunity, I decided to walk to ACI the following morning. As I strolled along, centering my thoughts and enjoying the architecture of Manhattan, the clouds overhead suddenly darkened and it began to pour. I had no umbrella and there was not a taxi in sight. By the time I reached Joanne's Third Avenue office building, I was completely drenched.

Joanne had only just moved into a new suite. Both her furniture and staff had not yet arrived. Despite my soggy condition, however, I was not about to let anything else dampen my excitement.

As the rain whipped against the large windows, Joanne, Sandy, and I sat on ACI's newly carpeted floor and discussed the idea of selling my products on air.

"You must understand," I began, "as a matter of principle, I cannot sell my cosmetics without being able to teach viewers how to properly use them. That has always been my philosophy." I explained. "It is precisely that knowledge that empowers women to look and feel their most *confident.*"

They nodded.

"Instead of just selling makeup, I would like to create a 'confidence kit,'" I said, carefully explaining to them my concept.

"Each kit shall be comprised of a small palette of color—four eyeshadows, two lipsticks, blush, lip pencil, and foundation—each of them neutral enough in tone to ensure that any woman of any color or ethnicity may use them."

"How will they know how to use the products?" asked Sandy.

"I shall also include a detailed face chart with ten easy steps for application. This way, each customer will understand precisely how to properly use them," I continued. "The diagram will include both a daytime and evening look and will remove the guesswork from applying makeup.

Sandy and Joanne became quite animated. They agreed that this idea was something I should indeed present to the Home Shopping Club.

"Perfume is also an important part of building that confidence," I added. "Wearing a beautiful fragrance is every woman's birthright. It puts air in one's tires. I wish to include a dram of my Pheromone in this 'kit' as well."

"The next step," Sandy advised, "would be for you to make a presentation to Ben White who heads Home Shopping's Celebrity Marketing division and the rest of his group, if you don't mind flying down to our corporate headquarters in Florida."

How could I say no?

On the flight home to Chicago, I jotted down notes to myself about an effective presentation to the board, deliberating as to which products should be included in my new Confidence Kit.

One week later, I left for Florida, scheduling a flight that would arrive early enough for me to enjoy a good night's sleep. I wished to ensure I would be fresh for my meeting the following morning at 9 a.m. Naturally, my plane was delayed, first because of mechanical problems, and then later, due to bad weather.

I did not depart Chicago until 11 p.m. and arrived in Tampa at four in the morning.

I checked into my hotel, removed all of my makeup, took a shower, dried my hair, and redressed. I had a quick breakfast and then departed for my presentation without having slept in over twenty-four hours.

No matter. A girl should always be well-prepared.

I presented my samples to the thirteen board members, all of them men. They were both intrigued and excited at the sales potential. Afterward, Ben White took me aside and asked me to accompany him to his office where we could speak privately.

"Marilyn, you might have something here," he began, quickly adding, "although you should know that we have no idea whether or not you would be accepted as an on-air personality. We never know how anyone will come across on television."

"I would like to try, Mr. White."

"The only thing is," he continued, "you can't go on television selling such an expensive product when you're already selling it in Saks Fifth Avenue, Neiman Marcus, and all of those high-end department stores. You can't have both, Marilyn," he said. "You cannot have prestige and a core business on television. If you do go on to do our program, you'll have to kiss your Neiman Marcus business good-bye."

I thought about this for a moment. But that power that guides me so often led me forward, and I was determined. I was sure that this was a glorious opportunity.

Without hesitation, I answered, "Mr. White, I am a woman who has never understood why I cannot have a piece of cake and enjoy a bite of it. I have been in Neiman Marcus for ten years now, but I have never sold my products on television. I am willing to take that chance."

My Confidence Kit configurations were accepted for the program and I could not have been happier when I received an initial order for one-thousand pieces. I was also very, very nervous.

In June of 1992, I prepared to make my debut on the Home Shopping Club. Although my previous experience in modeling and show business lent itself well to television, I had never faced a live television camera for more than several minutes at a time. As my debut drew near, I discovered I was developing a classic case of stage fright.

Bob Circosta a Home Shopping sales trainer was kind enough to share a few pointers, but it was my friend Dorsey Connors, who gave me the best advice. Dorsey, who for many years hosted her own television show in Chicago, said: "Think of the red light as the man you love."

Eventually, it came time to sink or swim.

I appeared on Home Shopping for the first time with host Terry Lewis Mason, and despite my preparation, I found myself looking at *her* nearly the whole time rather then the camera. But then something marvelous happened.

A Chicago customer who happened to be watching the program, phoned in and proceeded to share a wonderful testimonial. She announced on-air to the viewing audience they would be hard pressed to find products of higher quality—that both my makeup and Pheromone would change their lives.

Suddenly, the telephone lines became jammed.

Although I had been allotted thirty minutes of airtime, my Confidence Kits sold out in twenty minutes!

It was quite an experience. I was elated at my success and quite relieved.

Unhooking my microphone, I floated from the set, down the hallway, and back to the green room, where the buyers and show director waited. At the least, I thought that they would congratu-

An early TV appearance promoting Pheromone

late me, and indeed they did so. My excitement turned to worry, however when they added, "We want five thousand more kits."

I did not have enough stock to fill such a large order, and it took me nearly nine months to create enough pieces to fill the order before I could return.

This time, in addition to my color collection, I offered a bottle of Pheromone eau de parfum. Much to my relief, I quickly sold out every piece of merchandise in a matter of moments.

I returned yet again three months later, then two months later, and soon became a regular on what is now known as the Home Shopping Network (HSN).

More important than sales, I found great joy and fulfillment through meeting so many women. I looked forward to listening

220

to these new customers sharing their positive experiences with my products on HSN's testimonial lines.

When my first sack of letters arrived, I was touched with the candor and honesty contained within each note. Many ladies shared with me their personal difficulties and ambitions. They sought advice, and invested the time to thank me for helping them feel better about themselves.

It has always been my customers who have allowed my success. Their satisfaction and happiness is above all the most important aspect of my business. Letters, phone calls, and comments such as those from my HSN ladies helped to assuage the daily difficulties of maintaining my company.

My wonderful ladies became my extended family. They sent photographs of their children and grandchildren, pets, and before and after shots using my cosmetics. They shared with me the inspiration they had received from my products, and how they had gained self-confidence through using them.

During one of my on air appearances, I received a testimonial call from a woman suffering from agoraphobia. She had not ventured outside her house for nearly three years, avoiding friends, family, and as many social situations as she could.

After watching my presentation on television, she had decided to order one of my Confidence Kits. It changed her life completely. She called to tell me of her new courage. Not only could she now face the outside world, she was also volunteering at a senior citizen center.

Her call struck a chord with other viewers who called to share their stories.

What these customers will never realize, however, is the fact that they have given me more than I could ever give to them.

Many of the department stores carrying my fragrances, however, did not share my excitement. Concerned the availability of Pheromone on television at HSN pricing could temper their own sales, many store buyers expressed frustration over lack of exclusivity. To alleviate their fears, I visited with each divisional merchandise manager and asked that they remain patient. To me, it seemed an obvious conclusion that reaching sixty-five million women each month would do nothing but promote awareness of my brand and therefore increase store sales.

In the end, my theory was proven to be correct. For every five women who watched me discuss my beautiful fragrances on-air, one of them actually made a purchase. Conversely, four of them would ask to sample the same fragrance in the department stores. Sales increased. What's more, each time I did another in-store appearance, the crowd of ladies who recognized me from television increased tenfold. As I traveled around the country, it became a wonderful opportunity, as well, to meet the HSN customers who had taken the time to write or call.

One year later, I was being touted as the Queen of Fragrance. No one in the world had sold more perfume via television than I had. At the urging of my HSN customers, I shared with them a new fragrance I had developed called Magic. It became a best seller and women could not seem to get enough of it.

My cologne, M, which I created for the man who thought he had everything was introduced to great success. It also afforded me the opportunity to share my son on-air with viewers.

Shortly after graduating from college, Duke embarked upon a career in acting. Cast in independent feature projects, theater and television, it seemed a logical step for him to join me on camera. He demonstrated to the audience the "Ritual of the Male," a fragrance application technique used by ancient warriors before entering battle.

Duke was a hit. The ladies loved him and he returned to HSN often when M was being offered.

As sales for my cosmetics and fragrances continued to climb, I searched for an opportunity to also share my skin care products. Although I was told that skin care on the network was already saturated with competitors, I had no doubt that if allowed to present a unique line of products infused with the latest scientific technology, my passion and knowledge could impact the lives of millions of customers.

I began working with the department of dermatology at the University of Southern California. After negotiating an approval from HSN to proceed, we developed a unique, patented delivery system based upon the benefits of oxygen. The initial results were astounding.

In fact, the chief dermatologist at USC, Dr. Moy, was so impressed with the formulations, he urged me to have them patented. This is, of course, no easy feat. However, so confident was I about these new products, that I agreed to invest the necessary finances in order to begin clinical studies to *prove* that I had developed the most effective products then available in the marketplace.

Upon my second anniversary appearance at HSN, the Perfect Balance PDS (Patented Delivery System) line debuted, shattering all sales records for the network. In short order, my skin care products surpassed those of my cosmetics and fragrance. I had achieved my goal of making beauty possible for every woman and man. They now had the opportunity to enjoy products of the highest quality that many were otherwise unable to afford.

My participation on television ushered in a new era for me. Again, I had reinvented myself and my business, and again I had broken new ground in doing so.

It should be said that appearing on television is not as easy it may seem. Viewers are never aware of what transpires behind-the-scenes in producing a successful show. For two to three

On the Home Shopping Network with Terry Lewis Mason

hours at a time, I am the center of attention. During that period I must remain meticulously conscious of every movement I make and every word I utter.

Although it may not be apparent, on-camera appearances necessitate the use of a small ear piece which feeds directly to the director's control room. Should I use a word or phrase that may conflict with HSN legal guidelines, a voice in my ear chastises, "You cannot say that. Say this instead. . . ."

Once, an unexplained technical phenomenon delivered a Spanish channel into my ear piece. As I struggled to maintain my composure on-air, attempting to interact with the hostess and speak about the features and benefits of the product being sold, several people continued their Spanish conversation in my ear.

My grandmother always told me never to laugh uncontrollably in public. On occasion, however, I have not been able to help myself.

One such occasion occurred very early one morning, following an extravagant party that HSN had hosted for their on-air guests. Unfortunately, I was the one who had to return to the studio that evening for a midnight show.

Certainly I never drink before any appearance, but in the spirit of the event, I enjoyed a glass of champagne. That, combined with the fact that I had been up since four o'clock that morning contributed, no doubt, to the fact that upon returning to the set, I became quite sleepy. I tried valiantly to stay awake during the first few moments of the show.

As the show progressed, I noticed from the corner of my eye a preview for a "hanging" heart basket on the monitor. For whatever reason, I suddenly blurted, "Oh, look, Michelle! There's a hanging heart coming up!"

This may not seem funny upon reading it in print, but somehow, at that particular moment, it struck me as absurdly amusing and I began to laugh aloud.

Michelle Lau, the hostess, had no idea what I was referring to. She looked at me blankly and asked, "A hanging heart? What's a hanging heart?"

As I continued my effort to muffle my laughter, however, she became caught up in the giddiness of the situation and began laughing as well. After a few moments, I could not speak coherently and Michelle was doubled over in hysterics.

The director cut to a commercial until we could regain our composure, but in order to do so, we walked to opposite sides of the set, unable to look at each other for fear of instigating another fit of laughter.

During another show, I inadvertently hooked the heel of my shoe on the bar under a stool upon which I was sitting. Leaning forward to reach for a product, my foot caught and I toppled forward into the camera. I regained my composure as quickly as possible, smoothed out my suit and addressed the viewers.

"You know I happen to be very good at creating lovely fragrances. There are times, however, that I experience a slight difficulty in standing up."

The crew exploded with laughter.

It is, of course, one thing to fall down on camera and quite another to have a hostess nearly crash into you when she was stung by a bee. Then there was the time when I spilled a bottle of water, which trickled slowly down my leg while I struggled to remain in control and continue with my presentation as if nothing had happened.

Another time, I unbuttoned my short, tight skirt, pulling it down a bit to cover my knees when the camera focused on me sitting down. At some point, during a testimonial call, I became so excited, I stood up, forgetting that the buttons to my skirt were open. Only quick-thinking on the part of the cameraman who cut to a close up of my face kept my modesty intact that evening.

Never have I missed a show— despite being ill.

One evening, I joined a group of people for dinner at Pepe's, a Cuban restaurant near the HSN studios. That evening, it was suggested that I sample the shrimp, prepared in a special Cuban way.

"Why not?" I thought. It was delicious.

In the middle of the night, however, I awakened to a most unusual experience. Terribly ill, I did not think that I would live to see morning. Nothing stayed down. Not aspirin, not Alka Seltzer—nothing. After retching for hours, I became so dehydrated that I could barely stand. Finally, I managed to get dressed and met my driver in the hotel lobby.

"You may have to stop along the way," I advised.

Sure enough, I did have to get out of the car along the high-way. My stomach refused to be quieted. By the time we reached the HSN studios, I was still violently ill and needless to say, extremely weary.

Yet, the show must go on.

A clever producer gifted me with a bucket lined with plastic bags and positioned it just out camera range. "Don't worry," they assured me. "We'll cut away if you have to use it."

That was one of the longest days of my life.

Although Marlena and Duke were relatively unfazed by seeing their mother on television, Lee never missed a single show and always called to congratulate me when I returned to the hotel. Helen kept abreast of my appearances as well. True to character, she peppered her comments with brutal honesty.

"You know that suit you wore?" she would say. "Get rid of it."

During one visit to HSN, a woman approached, asking if I would ever consider traveling to Canada to discuss appearing on a Toronto-based network called The Shopping Channel. "I've been watching you on HSN and I'm impressed. I think you'd be wonderful on our network as well," she said."

Never one to refuse an opportunity, I agreed to meet with the TSC executives and subsequently began sharing my products with the women and men of Canada as well.

The Shopping Channel, lacking a proper license, and prohibited by Canadian laws from featuring any live motion during broadcast sales. Therefore, rather than traveling to Toronto for every show, on occasion I was able to telephone the studio from the comfort of my own office in Chicago. A technician patched my call in with the show host, who interacted as though I were in the studio with her. Rather than actually seeing the two of us, Canadian viewers listened to our voices and watched still photographs of my products and of the hostess and me.

In 1996, The Shopping Channel was able to obtain anew license, and I began traveling to Toronto monthly to appear live on camera.

As my reputation for excellence in the beauty industry was relatively unknown to TSC viewers, the business I developed there, and my Canadian customers in particular, became very special to me. Toronto became a home away from home, and I still look forward to visiting each month.

As my television appearances continued over the years, recognition of my name increased. Being well-known sometimes brings with it some interesting experiences.

One afternoon following a meeting at my corporate office, I walked outside to hail a taxi back to my Oak Street Institute. I did not have to wait long. In fact, I did not have to raise my hand. As I stepped to the curb, a yellow cab came racing down the street and screeched to a halt in front of me. Before I could even move, the driver's door burst open, followed by a man waving his arms frantically.

"Marilyn Miglin!" he shouted. "I just knew it was you! I *knew* it! What an honor it is to have you ride in my cab," he exclaimed, stepping around the vehicle to open the door, as if escorting me to a private chariot.

"I am proud to drive you, Mrs. Miglin," he said once I was inside the car. He continued to chat with me during the entire trip back to the salon. "I just can't believe it's really you! I carry samples of your fragrances in my car and give them to my fares when I can," he said. "I tell everyone coming into town from O'Hare that you live in Chicago. We sure are lucky to have you here," he boasted. "You do so much for the city."

"Oh my," I managed to reply. "Why, thank you."

Upon reaching our destination, he swerved the cab to the wrong side, against traffic.

"I can't let you walk *across* the street to get to your store, Mrs. Miglin. Now you can just step out onto the sidewalk."

When I attempted to extract the fare and a tip from my purse he shook his head. "Oh, no!" he refused. "I can't take money from Marilyn Miglin. It's *my* pleasure to drive you. What until I tell my wife and kids that I had you in my car today!"

Increasingly, I am recognized more and more. During dinner in Paris one evening, I was surprised upon being approached by a couple at the next table. "Aren't you Marilyn Miglin?" they asked. My daughter Marlena, who was with me, nearly dropped her fork.

In the spring of 1996, Alderman Burton Natarus telephoned my office to inform me that Chicago's City Council had voted unanimously to erect honorary signage on Oak Street.

"Chicago would like to pay tribute to you for not only your work on behalf of the Oak Street Council, but for your civic, philanthropic, and business efforts as well," he said. "There's no better way to do that than to christen Oak Street as 'Marilyn Miglin Way.' That street really belongs to you."

I was deeply touched.

The entire Oak Street Council could not have been more supportive of this special honor. I could not believe the reality of such prestigious recognition until the very morning Chicago's Department of Streets and Sanitation installed the actual signage on either end of Oak Street.

That afternoon, a veritable who's who of business and civic leaders, and many of Oak Street's retailers and property owners, stood beneath the now-veiled street sign, listening to

Being inducted into the Entrepreneurship Hall of Fame

Alderman Natarus' recitation of the City's official proclamation.
I was moved beyond words.

With the pull of a string, the new sign was revealed to a roar
of approval and applause. At my side, Lee positively beamed with
pride.

Local television crews and print media followed the crowd
that had gathered, across the street to my salon, where a small
celebratory luncheon had been planned. That day, I spent a good

deal of time thinking back to the challenges I had endured and the victories enjoyed over the previous thirty years I had invested in developing my business.

Further reflection reminded me that good times become good memories and bad times become wonderful lessons. There is always something positive and good in each experience. One can never lose. In life, we have everything to gain.

Of all the honors bestowed upon me, however, the most meaningful and certainly the most unexpected was the Raoul Wallenberg International Humanitarian Award.

When the local chapter of Jerusalem's Shaare Zedek Hospital contacted me with news that I had been selected as the 1997 honoree, I was stunned.

"There must be some misunderstanding," I replied, somewhat embarrassed. "You see, I am not Jewish. I'm Catholic. Besides," I added, "most of the philanthropic work I have contributed has been here in the United States—not internationally."

"Oh, no," laughed Barry Axler, the jovial rabbi who headed Shaare Zedek's Chicago offices. "Let me explain."

As it turned out, the award was not based upon religion or nationality, but rather on commitment to humanity.

"This is a very special award named for an extraordinary man," Barry said. "Raoul Wallenberg was not Jewish either. He was an amazing man who relinquished his own life to save one-hundred-thousand Hungarian Jewish children from the Nazis. Raoul Wallenberg said, 'If you save the children, you will save the nation.' That philosophy has always been an integral part of your own work and the efforts you've made in improving the lives of so many women, men, and children."

Listening to Rabbi Axler share with me the life and heroism of Raoul Wallenberg, and the ultimate sacrifice he made for others brought tears to my eyes.

"The award is given in two parts—a dinner here in Chicago, and then a tribute in Jerusalem at the Shaare Zedek Medical Center. All of the proceeds raised from the award dinner benefit the Raoul Wallenberg Pediatric Day Hospital, where all children are treated for illnesses and injuries regardless of their race, nationality, or religion. Given your passionate commitment to burn survivors, we would like to earmark those funds for a desperately needed pediatric burn unit to be established in your name.

"As an honoree, you're in good company," Barry continued. "People such as Miep Gies, the woman who hid Anne Frank and her family during World War II, and Isser Harel, who led the operation that captured Nazi war criminal Adolf Eichmann, are past award recipients."

I managed to reply, "I am honored. I don't know what to say!"

"Say you'll accept the award!" laughed the rabbi.

"Yes," I said. "I will."

A few months later, I worked with Barry to arrange an elegant pre-award reception at my home. Many friends and associates gathered to share a beautiful evening, and learn more about the mission of Shaare Zedek and Raoul Wallenberg. But it was violinist Victor Aitay, who lent a new meaning to the word "inspiring."

As First Chair Violinist Emeritus for the Chicago Symphony Orchestra, his supreme musical talent has affected millions worldwide. What many did not know, however, was that Victor happened to be one of the children saved from Nazi concentration camps by Raoul Wallenberg.

When Mr. Aitay stepped into my living room with his violin and began to play the haunting theme from *Schindler's List,* the entire room was overcome with emotion. When he finished, there was silence.

Before us stood a shining testament of Raoul Wallenberg's legacy, a living example of the difference one human being can make in changing the lives of many.

Never had I been so inspired and touched.

On April 8, 1997, eight-hundred guests filled the elegant Gold Coast ballroom of the Drake Hotel. On each table rested stunning eight-foot tall sculptures, each of them holding a multitude of votive candles. When the lights were dimmed, each candle twinkled high overhead like the proverbial night of a thousand stars.

I entered the ballroom with Lee. I was overcome at the presence of so many close friends, family, and business associates who had come to honor me. People representing every aspect of our lives were there to share this special evening.

In everyone's life there is a time—one precious moment so special—that it becomes transcribed in your memory to be cherished, enjoyed, and never forgotten. Everyone whom Lee and I cared about was present. There had been twelve people at our wedding thirty-eight years before. That evening, it was as though Lee and I were renewing our vows—as though that special night was the wedding celebration that Lee and I never had. Never have I been so happy.

The children of Ogden School were there to sing for me and after a touching video tribute was shown, I was called to the podium and presented with an exquisite crystal award. When I saw that inside the block of crystal there was a three-dimensional hologram of a beautiful angel. I was speechless. Rabbi Axler had shared with Oak Street jeweler Lester Lampert, who had designed the award, my passionate belief in angels and their symbolism.

At the Raoul Wallenberg International Humanitarian Award dinner

Choking back tears, I asked that each of those present reflect silently in honor of Raoul Wallenberg before lighting candles that had been placed in front of them. The entire ballroom fell silent.

Then the orchestra began playing a hora, the traditional dance of Israel. Lee led me to the floor and we began to dance, reaching out to those around us to join in as we passed their tables. Soon, the floor was filled with people, twirling in a circle, hands held tightly together in love, friendship, and renewed hope.

It was a magical evening—one of the proudest moments in my life, and one that I shall never forget.

When I returned to Home Shopping the following week, I brought my award to show my ladies. I shared with them my positive feelings about angels, which had been part of my life since childhood, and reminded my audience of that special presence all around us.

"Angels inspire us to embrace life's positive energy and dance with it. If we don't learn to dance on earth," I reminded them, "whatever will they do with us when we reach heaven?"

I know now, that as I continued my on-air appearances during that visit, angels were indeed looking down upon me.

CHAPTER TEN

A day of unbelievable darkness

Having broken yet another sales record at the Shopping Channel in Canada, I called Lee to share with him my excitement.

The following Monday we were to embark upon a long-awaited journey to the Grand Canyon. I could not wait to return home, celebrate my victory with Lee, and plan yet another special vacation.

"I'm so proud of you," he said. "Get a good night's sleep and I'll see you bright and early at the airport tomorrow."

"I can hardly wait to see you tomorrow," I said. "I love you."

"I love you, too," were his last words to me.

That night I awakened with a start. I sat straight up in bed with a horrible, heavy, and painful pressure in my chest, and glanced at the clock. It was shortly past midnight.

Despite trying to relax and doze off again, I merely tossed and turned. I had a feeling of desperation I could not understand. For some strange reason, I experienced an overwhelming desire to be home at that very moment. It made no sense. I continued to restlessly adjust and readjust my bed linens, looking at the clock every fifteen minutes to gauge the time when I could leave for the airport and take the first flight home at 6:30 a.m.

At 4 a.m., I arose, dressed, and checked out of my hotel. But even during the drive to the Toronto airport, I could not shake the foreboding I had.

What followed was the darkest day of my life, a day of unfathomable pain and sadness which shattered my fairy tale existence.

The return flight to O'Hare International Airport seemed to take twice as long as usual. Upon landing, I was the first passenger off the plane.

I could think of nothing more than falling into the reassuring arms of my husband as I always had, every time he met me at the airport. Lee never missed a flight. He was always there to greet me at the gate.

This time, he was not there.

I waited for a moment, thinking that perhaps he had walked across the terminal for a newspaper. It was uncharacteristic for him not to be standing there.

After waiting a few minutes more, I picked up a telephone and called his car phone. To my dismay, I was greeted with the message, "The number you have dialed has been transferred. . ." This was unusual, given the fact that we had utilized that phone number for years.

Again, I was overcome with a feeling of desperation.

I endured the long walk from the gate to the domestic terminal, all the while searching the crowd, hoping that I would see Lee coming toward me. Perhaps he had encountered unavoidable traffic on the highway.

As I rode down the escalator, I expected to see him ascending on the other side. Still, there was no sign of him.

With great apprehension and anxiety, I gathered my luggage and looked around the baggage claim area one last time before hailing a taxi.

It was the longest ride home I ever took.

There was no traffic on the expressway. No accidents. It was a bright, sunny morning with no signs of trouble that might impede a motorist's trip to O'Hare Airport. The entire way back, I knew that something was not right. Something had happened.

When we reached my driveway, the back gate was open and the kitchen blinds were not in proper order. Then I knew that something was terribly wrong.

I opened the door and called his name. There was no answer. The kitchen was in disarray. There were dirty dishes in the sink, something Lee would never leave for me. He was so neat and organized that he never left anything out of place.

Now I feared the worst.

Frantically shouting to him, I raced up the stairs to our bedroom. Perhaps he had suffered a heart attack or stroke. He could be alive but unconscious, and I would be able help him.

To my surprise, the bed had not been slept in.

In the bathroom, I noticed water in the sink and upon the vanity—a gun.

My heart felt as though it would explode. I stumbled down the stairs to call for help, fearing that the intruder might still be present. Fleeing from the house, I frantically ran down the alley looking for a public phone with which to call the police.

Walking toward me were my neighbors, Barbara and Steve Byers.

"Please!" I called out to them. "I need your help! Something's happened to Lee."

I ran back to the house with Steve, who bravely searched each room, floor by floor to see if anyone was there. He found no one.

Meanwhile, I telephoned the police and, upon reaching the Eighteenth District station house, asked to speak with Commander Ettore DiVito. He had always been a wonderful friend and had been present at the Wallenberg Award celebration only a few weeks beforehand. I was told that although Commander DiVito was indeed on duty that day, he was working a parade in another section of the city. Assuring me that the Commander would be notified as soon as possible, I was told that a squad car would be sent to the house immediately.

My next instinct was to see if Lee was in the garage. I didn't care if he were unconscious or not, I just wanted to find him.

The garage door opener was not where it should have been.

Pulling everything out of a drawer, I searched for the keys to the garage side door and ran back outside across the alley with the Byers. Steve stayed at my side, took the keys, and opened the garage. Lee's car was not inside. At that moment, I held firmly to the notion, hoping against all hope, that he had been kidnapped. Perhaps he was being held hostage in the car.

Again, I returned to the house and telephoned Lee's secretary, Nora, who lived down the street. She rushed over immediately.

Meanwhile, the Byers had gone back into the garage before returning to the house. The look of anguish on their faces confirmed my worst fear.

"Marilyn, he's dead," Barbara whispered.

The police searched the entire house, then reentered the garage. They found Lee behind his prized Bitter racing car.

As I ran back to the garage, an officer in the yard stopped me. "You cannot go in there," he insisted. "We've cordoned off this area. You'll have to see him at the morgue."

"No, I will not see him in the morgue," I protested. There was no way on God's earth that I would allow anyone to restrict me from going inside that garage. As I tried to push past the officer, another squad car pulled into the alley and Commander DiVito stepped out.

"Commander," I cried, "they won't let me see my husband. Please! I have to see Lee!"

"Let her go inside and see him," he said.

When I stepped into the garage, all time, all motion stopped. I could not breathe. My heart was wrenched from my body, and at that moment, my life was changed forever.

My beloved husband had been brutally murdered.

How could this be happening? What was I going to do? More squad cars arrived and within minutes, my once tranquil home was suddenly filled with scores of police officers and detectives combing every corner and dusting every surface for fingerprints. The atmosphere was pure bedlam.

When I was asked about the license plate of Lee's Lexus, I could not remember the number. It was as though I were floating in a heavy fog, the world around me spinning backward in slow motion.

At first it was difficult to comprehend what had happened. It was a living nightmare. Although I understood the events unfolding before me, I could not grasp the final reality.

With more law enforcement personnel sweeping every surface, they suggested that I leave the house.

"Please don't ask me to leave my home!" I pleaded. "It's my only point of reference. I have no where to go!" This was the house that Lee and I built together, and I was not about to allow anyone to force me out.

Again, Commander DeVito intervened. "Let her stay," he said. "She'll work with you."

With Nora at my side, I collapsed into a chair near the telephone. Duke was in California and Marlena was vacationing in Italy. What would I tell them? *How* would I tell them? More than anything else, I needed my children by my side.

When I picked up the phone to call Duke, it felt as though the receiver weighed ten pounds. My hands trembling, I could barely punch the numbers. I could not imagine what I would say to him.

Duke took the first flight back to Chicago and was home at my side five hours later.

In the meantime, there were others to notify. I called Helen and Aunt Virge. Then with a heavy heart, I called Lee's brother, Carl, who had idolized him as not only his older sibling but as a surrogate father figure.

My immediate family provided unconditional support and protection, but we struggled to make sense of what had happened.

A highly regarded businessman and civic leader beloved for his honor, professionalism, and unparalleled vision to shape Chicago's skyline, Lee's unexpected death was sudden news. In less than an hour, reporters were tripping over one another, erecting rows of tripods on the sidewalk across the street, each of them tightly focused upon the front door of my house. They swarmed the neighborhood, devouring any scrap of information, no matter how insignificant, from anyone they could find who had ever spoken to Lee.

The fact that most of those interviewed did not know him personally or anything about him, was apparently unimportant to the media. Obtaining the all-important sound-bite was all that mattered. Secondhand innuendo and the gossip it brought about were much more titillating. Broadcasting these rumors and unsubstantiated slivers of information provided each television station with an exciting newscast at my family's expense—the entire city of Chicago tuned in to watch the drama of my tragedy unfold.

Lee's brother Carl, immediately left his own home in Monticello and would remain with us in Chicago for many weeks to come.

Shortly after Duke's arrival, he began the challenge of contacting Marlena in Italy. For hours he called her friends and associates, desperately attempting to ascertain her whereabouts and a phone number where she could be reached.

Meanwhile, as friends and family heard the news, they rushed to the house to offer their consolation and support. Steve and Peggy Lombardo, the owners of Gibson's, one of Chicago's most popular restaurants, sent an enormous tray of food. The manager of the Palmer House Hilton Hotel sent platters of sustenance as well. Although we very much appreciated the kindness, no one could eat.

Reporters lined up outside did their best to capture any scrap of footage possible of those who entered my home. One local station even went so far as to set up a telephoto camera in a neighboring high-rise in order to ensure their evening broadcast included footage of the grieving widow in tears, pacing the floor of her kitchen. The invasion of my privacy and that of my family combined with the media's lack of respect during our deepest moment of grief was unconscionable.

Upstairs, the police had sealed off every room, leaving me the use of my bedroom and one bathroom, which I cleaned. The police had impounded my remaining car for fingerprints, leaving me with no transportation, my home had been invaded, and there were people everywhere in my kitchen.

Finally, Duke reached Marlena, who made the necessary arrangements to take the first available flight from Italy. She would arrive the following day.

When everyone but family finally departed, I was as alone as I ever would be for the next six weeks. Together, Duke, Carl, and I wept quietly.

That evening, I slipped into my empty bed, wondering if the day's events had been a dream. It seemed impossible to me that Lee was not there beside me. I wanted to do more than close my eyes that night. I wished to shut out the entire world.

Before turning out the lights, I lit a candle for Lee and placed it beside the bed. Then I cried myself to sleep.

It was my practice each day of awakening to the voice of Chicago radio broadcaster Felicia Middlebrook. The following morning was no different with the exception of WBBM radio's lead story. "A terrible tragedy has happened in Chicago's Gold Coast," she began.

I had hoped and prayed that the previous day was nothing more than a nightmare—that I would awaken in Lee's arms. Felicia's delivery of the morning news, however, shattered that fantasy, dragging me back to reality.

I staggered from bed, dressed, and went downstairs. So many people had gathered in the house that morning. Operating on autopilot, I did something Lee had always done every morning of our married life. I squeezed fresh orange juice for my family. I had to do *something* that would help me focus.

Nora returned to the house that morning and together, we prepared Lee's obituary, submitting it to the newspapers.

Flowers and more food arrived from everywhere.

Each chime of the doorbell signaled the arrival of yet another friend or member of the family who needed to share their feelings of shock and sympathy. Every time I answered the door, however, the sight of the news cameras positioned across the street was unavoidable.

In my kitchen, I numbly surveyed the vast array of food that remained untouched.

"Those reporters outside have been standing there for hours," I observed aloud. "They must be hungry."

There was more food than we could possibly eat, and it seemed a shame to let it go to waste. So, I sent a tray of sandwiches to the press stationed across the street. Needless to say, I was stunned and disappointed when this trivial event was reported upon within the hour.

Upon contacting a funeral home, I discovered that before Lee could be released to their care, his body needed to be identified. Duke and Carl drove to the morgue and saved me the pain of doing so.

Marlena arrived home from her exhausting and traumatic trip from Italy. She had been so close to her father and was completely devastated. I held her and together we sobbed.

During a rare, quiet moment with my son and daughter, I told them that apparently it had been time for their father to leave. We were not to judge the manner of his death, but instead celebrate his wonderful life.

Finally, the police detectives briefed us as to what they learned. A jeep parked just a few blocks from my home had gone unnoticed for several days. An overabundance of parking tickets accumulating upon its windshield finally caught the attention of the local law enforcement. A routine check on the vehicle's registration traced the ownership to a young man in Minneapolis who, along with a friend, had been murdered the previous week. The evidence pointed to a man named Andrew Cunanan, whom the police suspected had taken their lives before fleeing in the stolen jeep. He was mentally unbalanced and desperate to escape, and they believed he then drove to Chicago, looking for another car.

Several neighbors had observed Lee washing the Lexus that afternoon and tinkering in what should have been the safety of our own garage.

This fugitive parked the jeep, killed my husband, and then fled in his car. Simply put, Lee was the random victim of a sociopath in need of another vehicle with which to escape from the authorities.

I could not fathom how one person could be so selfish as to take the life of another. What gave him the right?

The grief I felt in my heart left me wondering if I could ever again experience happiness. The fact that the police and FBI now knew who they were looking for and were confident that the suspect would be apprehended did nothing to change the fact that Lee had been senselessly taken from us. Nothing could lesson the nightmare.

His death shocked the entire city. It became an event which touched everyone, reminding them, "There go I, but for the grace of God." It was something that should never happen to anyone and the compassion shared by so many people proved it.

Lee was not an ordinary man. I rediscovered this over and over again following his death. Strangers approached the children and me to share with us their respect for him and the kindnesses he had performed. His business associates' eyes welled with tears as they explained to me how Lee had mentored them. I discovered that he had helped support entire families in financial turmoil, as well as quietly performing many other unselfish acts.

Why had I not known of these generosities he had performed so long ago? Because he made sure that they were performed without attention, recognition, or reward—because he was a thoughtful, kind, and insightful man who felt that he should share his good fortune with others.

One of those touched by Lee's generosity and caring was my childhood priest and friend, Father Fu, who had married us. To assist him in realizing his lifelong wish, Lee purchased a building on the north side of Chicago and gifted Father Fu with the means to establish a Chinese Catholic mission house. He never forgot Lee's kindness.

The following morning was the one I dreaded most. After a family mass, Helen, my aunts Marion and Virge, Duke, Marlena, and Carl accompanied me to the cemetery, where our ninety-four-year-old Chinese priest prayed with us.

Father Fu did his best to comfort us in our grief, but he became so overcome with his own pain that he fell upon the casket, unable to control his sobs of anguish. It was then necessary for me to comfort my own priest.

"There is a beginning and an end to all lives," I told Marlena and Duke. "We may not understand why that ending comes when it does, but there is a reason for everything. You father gave us a positive outlook. Honor him now by carrying on with his strength and dignity."

It was terribly difficult to return to the house that evening, and I decided to take my family for dinner at Twin Anchors—a favorite restaurant of ours. Upon entering, I realized for the first time that for days, my face had been on every television station and in every newspaper in the city.

Everyone turned around in their seats to stare at me. People pointed and whispered to one another, and then they turned their heads the other way rather than meeting my gaze because they did not know what to say.

On Friday, May 8, we held a memorial at Holy Name Cathedral. It was a beautiful service and the church was filled to capacity with family and friends. The final of many tributes paid to Lee that day was the organist playing the Air Force Theme in his honor.

I knew that weeping publicly would do my family and me no good. We held our heads high and thanked the many hundreds of people who had joined us to celebrate Lee's memory.

I did my best to keep smiling. The more you smile, the more you stand up straight, the more your body remembers what life was like before you were unhappy. You can walk around with a broken heart, but you still must walk.

Lee was an incredibly strong and centered man, and the manner in which he conducted his life became a major influence in how we lived as a family. I could either crumble or put my best face forward, refocusing to get through the day and do what needed to be done.

Had I chosen the easier road, which would have been total collapse, my family and my company would then have *two* problems.

There were others who needed me, including my employees, who had their own obligations such as tuition, car payments, and families to support. These people looked to me for guidance and strength, and it was my responsibility to ensure them that they would be safe, that my company would indeed go on.

Following the service, I called my staff together, determined to stay as focused as possible. The more turmoil you have within, the more turmoil and confusion you project to those around you.

At some point during that first week, a friend had sent to me an ancient Egyptian bronze feather with the inscription: "Float above the turmoil like a feather in the wind, yet maintain the strength of forged bronze tempered with the wisdom of the ages."

Bronze feather in hand, I shared this with my staff and assured them that the business would indeed go forward.

Lee's life had touched each of them on many levels. When he entered my corporate offices or the Oak Street salon, people stood straighter and held their heads higher—not out of intimidation—but from genuine admiration and respect.

I would discover that many of my staff confessed to not only experiencing nightmares, but difficulties in sorting out their own emotions. When I shared this with a client who also happened to be a therapist, she graciously offered her counseling services to them.

I became the wounded who derived a sense of healing and peace by helping others. As the events surrounding Lee's death continued to unfold, this became my role.

I understood that I needed to go forward. I still had my children. I still had my mother and my elderly aunts. I still had my husband's family and many friends from whom I could draw strength.

The heartfelt condolences and poignant memories of Lee shared by so many helped to provide a cushion of support, but among the many messages I received, one in particular touched my heart considerably.

Michael Jordan's mother, Deloris, whom I had never before met, called to share her own wisdom and strength.

"I want you to know that I understand what you're going through. Two boys killed my husband for his car," she said. "I want to tell you to ignore the chaos around you. You'll get through this, but you must be strong and keep going for your family."

I would soon discover just how strong I needed to be.

Only hours after the memorial, the news wires reported that they had found Lee's car abandoned in a New Jersey cemetery, near the body of a caretaker, whose truck was now missing.

It had happened again.

The telephone began to ring and the swarm of reporters previously stationed outside the church earlier that morning, returned to their positions in front of the house, this time in greater numbers and with even less respect for our privacy.

We were dumbfounded. A media frenzy exploded in reporting every lurid detail of this newest murder. The caretaker had been a young man and left behind a wife and a two-year-old son. My first thought was that my own children had been fortunate in reaching adulthood before losing their father. Yet another family had been shattered by tragedy and grief. My heart ached for them.

Random violence triggers feelings of vulnerability. People have an almost visceral need to find a reason for such an act, to nail down a motive, and transfer the blame. The media chased this newest development with rabid zeal and stepped up it's relentless pursuit of *anyone* willing to speak with them.

In the midst of this bedlam, I somehow rediscovered a strength, something I realized was an inherent part of my own faith. It was an inner voice that said: "You can get through this day and go on to the next."

When Duke had been accepted into the Air Force Academy, many years previously, his commanding officer came to personally greet him and our family.

Since Duke was only sixteen years old at the time, the Air Force required Lee and me to relinquish his guardianship to the charge of the U.S. Government.

The colonel waited patiently as we embraced our son and then announced that there were to be no more family good-byes.

"I'm going to give you the most important advice you're ever going to receive, young man," he addressed Duke. "It won't hurt you to hear it either," he added, turning to Lee and me.

"Take ten minutes at a time. Get through those ten minutes and you can get through an hour. If you can get through an hour, you can get through two."

I thought a lot about that advice and did my best to follow it.

Accepting the obligations of each day necessitated returning to work, although I knew it would not be easy for me or those around me. I had a business and a street to run and I could not relinquish my responsibilities.

On the first day of my return, I walked to the office as I had always done. The people who usually greeted me each morning were shocked at my presence on the sidewalk. They did not know what to say. It was terribly difficult to maintain a smile, knowing that my very presence caused such a level of discomfort to those around me. I was determined to let them see that I had not collapsed.

That afternoon, I presided over the monthly meeting of the Oak Street Council, as I had always done. As the Board quietly made their entrance into my office, the air was thick and awkward. Their struggle in finding the precise words to express their sorrow and concern was painfully obvious to me.

After accepting their initial greetings and condolences, I calmly read aloud the meeting's agenda. Upon realizing that I intended to proceed with business at hand, they relaxed considerably, immediately comforted in knowing that "Marilyn was back at the helm."

It was another example of the wounded helping to heal the pain and discomfort of others in order to heal herself. Rather than taking to my bed, my presence helped to quell the initial discomfort of others.

People asked if my family and I were finding any closure. This was a question I continue to struggle with. What is "closure"? How does one find any closure when enduring a tragedy so public?

Each day, the press breathlessly reported upon the events of an increased manhunt to find the assailant authorities now described as a spree killer. It was apparently unimportant to the media circus stalking my neighborhood that as the FBI continued their search, there was no relevant information to share. This void of any new "juicy" details, coupled with the sensationalistic nature of the crimes, fueled intense speculation about any connection between perpetrator and victims.

My family, my friends and my employees were hounded by reporters for further information that did not exist. Those closest to us regarded the temptation of appearing on the local news as insulting and the media itself as an intrusion.

Lee's killer was upgraded to the FBI's Ten-Most-Wanted list of fugitives. The story was now national news and we found ourselves in every publication from *Time* to *People* magazine.

Rumors ricocheted around the country. Hurtful innuendo and speculation heaped more pain upon grief for not only my family and me, but for the other families who struggled valiantly to move forward with their own lives.

In the midst of this continuing nightmare, I had another painful decision to make. I agonized over my previously scheduled monthly appearance on the Home Shopping Network.

If I proceeded with plans for my scheduled visit, I knew that there would be those who would question my integrity, ready to launch personal attacks on my character for appearing on television so soon after the death of my husband. As a businesswoman, however, I felt that I had an obligation to fulfill. I also needed to keep busy—anything to keep my mind off the turmoil surrounding me.

During those first three weeks, as the news of Lee's death became a national story, I received thousands of letters and cards of condolence from my HSN customers. I personally answered each and every note. It was emotionally draining, but also heart-warming and it helped to keep me focused.

If I did not return to television, I felt that everything I had always believed in so passionately would end. I was terribly concerned that those who looked up to me, those who praised my conviction and faith would think, "She fell apart. She really doesn't believe in the things she's talked about on television all these years. Marilyn's always telling us to be strong and we've tried to follow her advice. Now look at her."

After I had a heartfelt discussion with Marlena and Duke, they agreed with my determination not to allow adversity to affect my life or theirs. My family and my company offered their unconditional support in my ultimate decision to return to HSN as planned.

I boarded my flight to Tampa feeling more alone that I had ever felt in my entire life. As the plane taxied to the runway, however, I began to question my decision. I feared a breakdown. What if I became emotionally distraught in front of the camera?

HSN executives could not have been more accommodating. I was told, "If at any time you need to leave, if you need to walk off the set, just go."

When the time came for my first show, I struggled to keep control of my emotions. But then I looked at the camera's red light, a symbol of the customers who had always looked to me for strength, and I heard myself say, "A terrible tragedy has occurred in my life. I have always believed that we must remain strong and proud for our families. You are all my extended family . . ."

I was taking those ten minutes at a time. With each painful hour of each painful day, I was surviving by demonstrating to others who were enduring their own private tragedies to do the same.

The response from my ladies was both positive and over-whelming.

During one of my shows, a woman called to offer a heartfelt testimonial on my skin care products. She told me and sixty-five-million viewers that her daughter was terminally ill with cancer. She had so much pain in her legs that she could not stand to be touched by anyone. There was nothing that anyone could do for her. "It's devastating to see my daughter this way," the caller shared. "So, I decided to bring your Iolight machine and skin care products to the hospital. I started applying them gently on her legs, Marilyn, and for the first time, my daughter found some relief from her agony."

I could barely maintain my composure. This lovely woman was trying to comfort me in the midst of her own grief. Her comments triggered deep emotions and I did have to momentarily leave the set.

When I finished my scheduled shows, including a return to the Shopping Channel in Canada, I breathed a sigh of relief. I was weary, but my deep well of faith and determination prevailed.

Naturally, the media reported my television appearance, but as details of the manhunt began to subside, a momentary lull provided the false illusion that we might return to some semblance of normalcy.

Part of me wished to believe that everything I knew was gone. Everything in my life had changed, I rationalized. Deep in my heart, however, I knew this to be untrue. The cup held in my hand was just as sturdy as when Lee drank from it. The table upon which I leaned still supported the weight of my elbows. I began to see that even though he had died, the world itself was familiar.

The danger for any widow is to use the loss of her husband to have contempt for the world. With grief comes the tendency to retreat into ourselves. By doing so, however, we become indifferent, unwilling to see color in any object, the good in any person, and meaning in our universe. The very word "widow" should be removed from our vocabulary and replaced with "survivor."

July signaled yet another return to Home Shopping. This second visit and the others that would follow, I reasoned, would become less difficult as time progressed. Though weary, I prepared for my departure with a renewed sense of optimism.

Little did I realize that there are some nightmares from which it is impossible to awaken.

I continued to find solace in hiding behind the camera. For several hours at a time while on set, the painful reality and challenges facing my family became a distant blur. We were surviving. But sometimes, fate has a way of testing our reserves.

Upon reaching my hotel on July 15th, I received an emergency call from Chicago. Fashion designer Gianni Versace had been gunned down in front of his Miami home by the same killer. The news and pandemonium that followed completely shattered any hope of calm in our lives. The entire world was shocked.

Although HSN's studios in Tampa were hours away from Versace's home in South Beach, the FBI insisted upon taking no chances regarding my safety. Agents escorted me to and from the set, the studio tightened its security, and FBI helicopters circled the skies overhead.

I was terrified.

A phone call from Marlena signaled to me that she had reached her breaking point. "Mom," she sobbed, "When is it ever going to *end*?"

How much more could we possibly take?

The tragic news of Versace's death merged with the story of what had become the most unsuccessful manhunt in U.S. history. It was now the lead story around the world.

A phone call from my salon confirmed the presence of dozens of cameramen positioned on Oak Street to photograph the entrance of Versace's Chicago boutique, which was, ironically, located directly across the street from my business. I could only imagine the cameras swiveling on their tripods from Versace's store to my own.

The *National Enquirer, Hard Copy, The Star,* and every other tabloid had already descended into our neighborhood in search of anyone who would speak to them about any of Andrew Cunanan's victims. A well-known television personality insisted that I appear on his show to discuss the events. *Good Morning America*, the *Today Show*, CBS, CNN, and *Newsweek* and *Time* magazines hounded my staff in their effort to speak to my family and me.

I could not understand it then, nor do I now. What was it they thought I would say?

"Marilyn might find some 'closure' in talking about her tragedy," reasoned the TV host to my assistant. The media never stopped to consider that their very presence in my life only added to the turmoil, reopening wounds, and snatching away the still fragile emotional superstructure to which my family and I were desperately clinging.

There was no shortage of others who were perfectly willing to be interviewed, eager for their own fifteen seconds of fame and glory before the television camera. It is curious how tragedy sheds new light upon those we know and have trusted as friends.

It was incredible to me that this assailant had managed to elude the authorities for two months. Despite the FBI's efforts to apprehend him, he seemed to repeatedly slip through their hands. Numerous sightings during those months were indeed frustrating but when Versace was killed, I was completely stunned.

Posters and bulletins proclaiming the fugitive to be a man of "a hundred faces" caused a furor and it became difficult to keep track of the potential validity of each new reported sighting. It took the discovery of stolen merchandise at a Miami pawn shop, including several gold coins taken from my home, for authorities to realize that he had, most likely, been interacting with the citizens of South Beach for days, possibly weeks, before coldly targeting his final victim.

The world waited breathlessly for the latest developments.

In the end, the killer was discovered aboard a vacant houseboat. By the time the police found him, he had committed suicide.

Why did he do what he did? How can one human being be filled with such disregard and malicious contempt for the lives of others?

He left no note behind and we will never know his motives.

It didn't matter. The outcome did not change the fact that Lee had been taken from us. It did not bring me peace, it did not bring closure.

I continued to reach out to a higher power seeking desperately to heal my heartache and that of my family.

No one could have lived the life I did with Lee Miglin. We enjoyed thirty-eight years of passionate romance, love, and adventure. I could not question God as to why things happened in the manner they did. Increasingly, I began to understand that I could only thank Him for the beautiful time I did have with Lee.

Cards and letters of condolence continued to stream into my home and office. I answered each of them before sending them to Lee's mother Anna in Westville. I wished for her to understand fully the impact her son's life had on so many.

One evening, while organizing another parcel of cards, I rediscovered the bronze feather previously given to me by an acquaintance. At first, I fought to hold back my tears, until I reread the inscription accompanying this gift.

I finished bundling the latest stack of cards and letters. Turning off the kitchen lights, I climbed the stairs, feather in hand and placed it along side the candle I kept burning for Lee next to my bed.

The sun arose the next morning as it always did. Upon awakening, I turned over to find that Lee's candle had burned down during the night. I then noticed the bronze feather beside it.

The beginning of a new day beckoned, begging to be embraced. With all the strength I could muster, I knew it was time to carry on.

CHAPTER ELEVEN

*I*t is said that there are measurable stages of grief, the first being disbelief. Perhaps it was exactly that emotion which made me think at times that any minute, I might awaken from my nightmare.

There were days when I felt I could not possibly go on. Ye t I did. Not because I was necessarily stoic or brave, but because there was simply nothing else I could do.

There were evenings that I went to bed and prayed I would wake up without having to remind myself to breathe.

I felt dazed.

It was if I were going through the motions of each daily activity like a robot. It felt as though all of my feelings had been frozen. The agony was unbearable, and I felt wounded, confused, isolated, empty, and alone. My heart was broken.

A sudden death—especially when life has been deliberately and maliciously taken—gives rise not only to the usual feelings of grief, but a whole set of other reactions. Friends and relatives quickly "burn out," leaving one without her usual support system.

To so many around me, however, the issue and the nature of Lee's death was difficult to get around. Acquaintances and customers squeezed by with, "How are you?" to which I replied, "I am not." Many shied away altogether, unable to face my pain.

"He's with God, so be strong," I heard time and again.

People said all the "right" things that somehow sounded wrong. I knew that they were hurting for me and doing their best to say anything they could to help ease my pain, but it was awkward. Those around me were also struggling with feelings they did not understand.

One strong shoulder on which Duke, Marlena, and I would come to rely was an old friend named Eugene Martello. I had known him for years, and while I presided over the Oak Street Council, Eugene served as president for the neighboring River North Association of merchants. Throughout the years, we sat together on various committees and often found ourselves working on common projects. He had adored Lee. While others were speechless, Eugene never shied away. He was always available, offering me the hand of compassionate friendship.

Somehow, he managed to consistently guarantee his presence whenever I felt I had reached a low point. Despite his caring and companionship, however, I felt as though I were in limbo much of the time—physically and emotionally exhausted.

Not a day went by that I stopped missing Lee. Particular dates, places, and activities sometimes sent me spiraling and brought back pain more intense than ever. Some days I hung onto my grief because it felt familiar and kept me close to him. Letting go at times seemed like an act of forgetting.

Gradually, I began to make a concerted effort not to look back. It was not easy.

In September of 1997, the City of Chicago dedicated a stretch of Madison Street in the Loop, which Lee had significantly developed, with honorary signage—Lee Miglin Way.

It was a fitting tribute to his passionate vision of dramatically shaping Chicago's magnificent skyline. Mayor Richard M. Daley was on hand to present the City's proclamation and I could not help but remember the pride that Lee exuded upon the dedication of my own honorary signage. Now it was I who found it difficult to hold back my emotion.

In the ensuing months, I did my best to concentrate on business and tend to the daily activities for which I was responsible. One project, in particular, to which I dedicated my efforts, was the impending launch of a new fragrance called Mystic. For many months, prior to Lee's death, he and I had spent considerable time discussing and adjusting the formulation. We developed Mystic's extension products, arranging for the packaging, and fine-tuning the marketing approach with which it would be launched.

Although I was not looking forward to the ensuing publicity, it was important to me to see the project through to the end.

In the meantime, Chanel, had built a beautiful new boutique on the corner of Michigan Avenue and Oak Street, anchoring our shopping districts. As the Oak Street Council president, my presence was requested at the new store's dedication ceremony and I was asked to help cut the ribbon. After initial hesitation, I agreed to do so, hoping that my attendance would not provide renewed fodder for the local gossip columnists.

Once again, I found myself in the company of Deloris Jordan, who had previously provided such dignified strength to my family and me.

As the other VIPs were ushered about on tours of Chanel's new facilities, Deloris and I found a quiet corner in which to chat.

"I think it's time for you to get back out into the world," she advised. "You need to become involved with something new."

When I explained my plans for the new fragrance, she raised a hand in front of her. "That's not what I mean," she said. "You need to become involved in something else outside your business. It would do you good, Marilyn."

Deloris went on to share with me the details of a gala dinner she had been asked to chair, honoring Marian Wright Edelman, a woman I had held in high esteem for many years.

Founder and President of the Children's Defense Fund (CDF), I greatly admired her passion and advocacy for disadvantaged Americans. Under her leadership, the CDF had become a national voice for children and families. Its mission to "leave no child behind" ensured a "Head Start" in life through this and other successful programs which benefited from its funding. I remembered well her involvement with Dr. Martin Luther King and how she had toured the nation's impoverished neighborhoods with Bobby Kennedy in the mid 1960s, drawing attention to the educational and developmental issues facing our children—*all* children.

"You know," I told Deloris, "I happen to have had my own experiences with the Head Start Program." As I went on to explain how my own children had benefited from Marian Wright Edelman's extraordinary vision and tenacity, I found myself becoming enthusiastic about the subject.

"Good," said Deloris. "That settles it. The purpose of this event is two-fold, to honor Marian and to raise money for the Children's Defense Fund. You will become a co-chair for this event. Hillary Rodham Clinton has already agreed to serve as Honorary Chair, and I'm working on getting Glenn Close to emcee the award dinner."

I swallowed hard, wondering what had just happened.

Only days beforehand, I had struggled with the decision to attend Chanel's ribbon cutting ceremony. Suddenly I found myself agreeing to co-chair yet another event with Deloris and Mrs. Clinton.

"I'll call you," said Deloris, before disappearing into the crowd of people.

A few weeks later, she did just that.

In short order, my office became the headquarters for weekly planning meetings with more and more people becoming involved. Between the forthcoming days spent fine-tuning plans for my newest fragrance and hours on the telephone attending to details of the Children's Defense Fund dinner, I had little time for anything else during the day.

The evenings were still the most difficult. After leaving the office, I returned to an empty house filled with memories. Duke and Marlena were home whenever possible, but they had their own lives to live.

Those quiet times by myself spent thinking and reflecting on the life Lee and I had shared were both joyful and terribly difficult. Everywhere I looked there was a photograph, an object, or a memento of some kind that reminded me of Lee, signaling a rush of emotion that I could not avoid.

At times I felt as though I were going mad, unable to control an unconscious barrage of images—of Lee and happier times juxtaposed against the constant reminder that he was no longer beside me.

During those times, it was Eugene Martello, who provided a respite of mischief and laughter to balance my erratic swing of emotions. Somewhere along the line, Marlena and Duke began referring to him affectionately as their eccentric "Uncle Eugene," a moniker that stuck. On the days that I did not look forward to going home, it was Eugene's uncanny radar that honed in on the situation without fail.

"'Miggy'," he chirped into the telephone, "I'm taking you, Marlena, and the 'Dukester' on a new adventure tonight. We're going to have dinner at an interesting Armenian restaurant I know of. They serve nothing but meat! Meat soup, meat sauce, meat bread, and for dessert—meat sorbet."

Eugene's outrageous sense of humor never failed to make me laugh aloud and break the monotony of those difficult times.

As the holidays approached, a new wave of emotions and melancholy greeted me. Early in our marriage, Lee had belonged to the Society of Industrial Realtors, which held a convention one year in Owahu. It was my first trip to Hawaii, which I thoroughly enjoyed. Remembering that one of my clients had raved about the serenity and beauty of Mauna Kea, we flew there and took a chance in asking if there were any rooms available. As luck would have it, there were.

We fell in love with Mauna Kea and for twenty-seven years, it became our family gathering place at Christmas. It was an annual tradition we all looked forward to.

In the end, there was absolutely no question that Marlena and Duke and I would travel to our special tropical paradise. Despite the fact that we needed to grieve with our Mauna Kea friends, it would have proven more difficult to have stayed home.

Vivid memories of more joyful times awaited us in Mauna Kea and we spent the holidays reminiscing—sharing family stories and special memories. The trip provided a renewed reserve of energy I needed in order to begin my first new year without Lee.

Back in Chicago, I decided to master something I had always wanted to accomplish—Spanish. I hired a personal instructor to tutor me at home during the early morning hours when I was unable to immerse myself with business calls. It provided not only a nice diversion to my grief, but enlightened and expanded my own outlook. In fact, when a Home Shopping producer heard that I was learning the language, she asked if I would be interested in appearing on an experimental new network, broadcast in Spanish.

I made my debut on Spanish Home Shopping, and although it did not last very long, I accomplished what I had set out to do.

Meanwhile, plans for the Children's Defense Fund dinner began falling into place. It was confirmed that Hillary Clinton would be attending the dinner and that Glenn Close would indeed be present to host the gala evening. There were security details, menus, publicity, and many other matters to plan and each time I met with Deloris, the event grew larger in scale.

Before re-emerging as a public personality, however, I needed another diversion to recharge my strength and emotional well-being. After I discussed with Duke a previously planned trip to the Grand Canyon, which Lee and I had looked forward to, my son and I decided to proceed with the itinerary. It was, we felt, exactly what Lee would have wished, and I personally looked forward to the spiritual beauty of Arizona's landscape.

Our mini-vacation did indeed boost my spirits.

The spectacular scenery of Sedona and its stunning red-rock spirals of sandstone were inspiring. The harmony of sacred Native American spirituality and the dramatic scenery were quite moving. There, I felt closer to the hand of God and drew increased strength and peace. Before driving north through the switch-backed mountain roads toward Flagstaff, Duke and I decided that an open-air plane tour was in good order. Climbing into a bi-wing three-seater plane, I pulled on a pair of airplane goggles, and was taken back to similar adventures of soaring high above stunning landscapes with Lee.

By the time we arrived at the Grand Canyon National Park, I felt weary from the whirl of emotions I had experienced in Sedona. Although we had reservations the next morning for a mule ride through the canyon, I ultimately decided that a quiet day of observing the sights from the safety of the south rim was more palatable.

The morning of our scheduled ride, Duke and I arose for an early breakfast, then proceeded to the park's ranger station to inquire as to whether or not it was possible for them to refund our money. Given the two-hundred dollar per person reservations, it was certainly worth the effort of attempting to recover the money.

Imagine my surprise when upon approaching the ranger in charge of the excursion, he bellowed at me, "Miglin? Where have you been! You're late and the entire group has been waiting for you!"

Before Duke or I could offer an explanation, he took me by the elbow and motioned me toward a mule.

"Why are you wearing black!" he hollered. "What's the matter with you? It's one-hundred-fifteen degrees in the canyon. Hurry up and get on that mule! We'll have to spray you down with water."

I looked to Duke for assistance in wriggling out of this embarrassing situation, but he merely shook his head. Personally, I think he felt that the spectacle of seeing his mother chastised in front of ten other tourists and the prospect of her being hosed down with water was quite amusing.

Given the circumstances, I could not help but laugh. I climbed onto the mule. I was doused with water and away we went, our caravan following the lead donkey.

Riding a mule is not one of the most comfortable activities I have enjoyed. As we approached the entrance to Bright Angel Trail, the ranger stopped briefly to issue a few words of solemn advice.

"The trail gets pretty narrow in some places," he warned. "These mules are no fools. In those areas, they will attempt to hug the canyon wall. When that happens, you'll have to swing your legs around to avoid being crushed."

I turned around atop my burrow and looked to Duke, who was listening intently to the ranger's directions.

"The other thing is this," he continued. "We'll be stopping for water and to rest the mules every forty-five minutes or so. I am riding the lead mule. When he stops, all the donkeys stop. Make sure that when they do, you use the reins to keep them facing the precipice. You want to ensure that they remember how high up we are. If they turn around toward the canyon wall, they could back up and you'll both go over."

The corners of Duke's mouth turned upward ever so slightly and I sighed a deep breath. There was no turning back.

Twenty minutes into the journey, the woman just behind the ranger began to cry, she was so terrified of the canyon floor over five miles below. "I can't do this," she sobbed. "I need to go back."

It was quite obvious to everyone in the caravan that this was impossible. Not only did the width of the trail prohibit anyone from turning around, there was no way that she could have handled the animal's ascension on her own, without the guidance of the ranger and his lead mule.

As this poor woman hung on for dear life, both arms wrapped tightly about the donkey's neck, she began to sob louder.

"Shut up, Lady! Just shut up!" called someone in back of me.

Someone else said, "We're all going down. It's too late now. Hang on, Honey, and enjoy the ride!"

Those were sound words of advice and I heeded them, holding tightly to the reins. Once I adjusted to the terrifying height, however, I began to enjoy the stunning vista. Although I did have to be watered down every so often to guard against the intense heat, and despite the fact that on our return to the canyon rim, walking was, shall we say, a bit uncomfortable, it was an unforgettable experience.

If the mule trip were not enough to sate our renewed appetite for adventure, the next day Duke and I decided to explore the canyon floor. Given the fact that there are two alternative means of transportation to the bottom—mule or helicopter—we opted for the latter.

It was our wish to visit Havasu Falls, a deep, spectacular gorge, where the Havasupai Indians had lived for hundreds of years. The photos in several of the tourist guides we had perused indicated the waterfall and the landscape to be truly breathtaking. Needless to say, I was quite relieved that *this* time, our descent into the Grand Canyon would be assisted with the comfort of modern technology.

Our helicopter did indeed take us safely to the bottom. However, I was not prepared for the horses that greeted us.

"Where are the Havasu waterfalls?" I asked.

"Oh, no," said the pilot. "The falls are nine miles away. You have to get there on horseback. We'll be back to pick you up in five hours," he smiled, climbing back into the cockpit.

Inwardly, I groaned. Again, Duke merely shook his head.

I adore horses and consider myself to be an accomplished rider, but as I was still recovering from our mule experience, the thought of mounting a horse was not an especially happy one.

"Well," Duke offered. "At least you're not dressed in black."

In the searing heat, our horses navigated the challenging trail until at last, we reached an open area. There, other riders were heading back onto the trail in the direction from which we originated.

"Where are the falls?" Duke queried one gentleman.

"You'll have to leave your horses here," he advised. "See those rocks over there?" he motioned. "There's an entrance to the gorge on the other side."

"A gorge?"

With Duke in Hualapai Canyon

"Yeah. You have to climb down about one-hundred-fifty feet to get to the falls. But don't worry," he added. "If you can't climb down, they can use a harness to lower you in and haul you up. Have fun," he said climbing atop his horse. "It's beautiful."

In silence, I watched him ride off on the trail. Before I could say anything to Duke, a woman rounded the bend of rock, pale and wheezing. It was not necessary to even ask if she were returning from the gorge.

"Did you see the falls?" asked Duke.

She nodded, attempting to catch her breath. "Beautiful," was all she said, before opening her canteen to guzzle water.

"We can turn around and go back, you know," Duke soothed me. "I don't mind."

That was it. We had come all that way and I wanted to see those waterfalls. Nothing, at that point, was going to stop me.

"Let's do it," I said.

The drop to the floor of the gorge did not seem to me to be that great a distance. The terrain necessary in maneuvering its depth, however, was indeed daunting. I could not imagine climbing down and back up, but I certainly was determined to do so.

The image of Marilyn Miglin climbing gingerly into a gorge is not something that I care to embellish upon; however, the unexpected challenges we endured in reaching Havasu Falls were well worth the effort.

There, at the base of the Hualapai Canyon, in an otherwise arid desert environment, lay a Garden of Eden. Under a canopy of shady cottonwood trees, the tumbling blue-green waters of Havasu creek and the waterfalls were among the most spectacular we had ever seen. Duke and I marveled at this hidden oasis and laughed upon further reflection of our difficulties in reaching it.

It should be mentioned that our laughter dissipated rapidly upon the thought of ascending the steep rocks in order to return to our horses above.

From Arizona, we flew to California, where Duke had been negotiating the purchase of a lovely piece of property. Lee had been working closely with him, offering his guidance and fatherly advice. He had been quite pleased over our son's first real estate transaction.

Upon Duke's finally closing the deal, a wave of satisfaction and peace came over me. It was as though Lee were smiling down upon us and nodding in support. After Duke signed the paperwork, we celebrated by toasting the memory of Lee—one year to the day he died. It was a very special occasion for not only Duke, but for me as well.

Our trip west had been exhausting both physically and emotionally. It did, however, help both of us on a number of levels—primarily spiritually. We hoped that we would finally be able to move forward with our lives again.

In April, I proceeded with plans to launch my fragrance Mystic at Marshall Field's. Print advertisements and city bus panels heralded its arrival, and I must admit to trepidation over the thought of supporting the launch with a series of department store appearances that would put me back in the spotlight.

I was truly honored when to celebrate the kickoff, the City of Chicago proclaimed April 15 as Marilyn Miglin Day. As previously anticipated, I found myself yet again on the front page of the *Chicago Tribune* in a story headlined: "One year later . . ."

That story triggered a new wave of interest in my tragedy and it wasn't long before *People* magazine, *Hard Copy,* and other tabloid shows called my office to ascertain my interest in dredging up the worst moment of my life. When a free-lance writer I had known for years asked to interview me for an uplifting piece detailing the success of my business for *Ladies Home Journal*, I reluctantly agreed, pleased with the prospect of positive PR that had nothing to do with the past year. I should not have been surprised when the one-page story served only to detail the drama of Lee's death.

The ensuing weeks were tremendously difficult with the challenge of successfully launching Mystic and renewed media attention. I did my best to maintain the dignity my grandmother had instilled in me and the quiet strength with which Lee lived his life.

Appearing on Home Shopping was one thing. Hiding behind the camera's red light, I was able to momentarily forget my grief. A personal appearance in a public department store was quite another. Yet, I could not help but be touched by the overwhelming display of positive emotion the customers and fans responded with as I stepped back into the limelight.

"Do you realize what an inspiration you are to other women?" I was asked. And to be truthful, that thought had never occurred me. I was besieged with well-wishes and testimonials from women who shared with me their own personal tragedies. They explained that I had given them hope, setting an example for others by putting my best face forward.

The evening of our Children's Defense Fund event finally arrived. Deloris and I were first briefed on security measures by the Secret Service before being introduced to Mrs. Clinton, who lent a lovely and inspiring presence of her own. Seated next to her on the dais, I watched as Marlena and Duke were photographed with then General Colin Powell, Glenn Close, and a plethora of other local and national celebrities who had gathered to honor Marian Wright Edelman. My children were perfect examples of the benefits from Marian's Head Start program. It gave me great pleasure to share with her how not only they had

With Deloris Jordan

prospered from her vision, but how much the other children at Ogden Elementary School had, as well.

As the gala drew to a close, I looked at a clearly exhausted but delighted Deloris Jordan, who returned my gaze with a smile.

Of course, she had known exactly what she was doing when she solicited my involvement for the event. The expression on her face spoke volumes and I shall be eternally grateful for her wisdom and insight.

That evening, my obligations fulfilled, I returned home, wondering what the next year would bring. It *had* to be better than what I had endured the previous twelve months. I carefully removed my makeup and dressed for bed with a sliver of renewed hope for the future.

CHAPTER TWELVE

*"No matter what fairy tales teach us, marriage does
not always go on happily ever after. But the memory
of love does stay with you forever."*

aving endured a year of darkness, I did not look forward to boarding a plane to Israel in order to accept the second half of my Raoul Wallenberg Award. The thought was overwhelming. Marlena and Duke, however, felt that it would be best that I go. It was an opportunity, they reminded me, to get away and carry on with what Lee and I would have done together.

After further reflection, I acquiesced. Both of my children expressed enthusiasm in accompanying me, and I felt that their presence would be of great comfort on the long trip.

My free-spirited daughter, who left three days earlier on her own sight-seeing itinerary, met Duke and me on June, 8, 1998. It was a long, restless flight to Jerusalem. We checked into our hotel rooms, quickly showered, and dressed for dinner. Downstairs, we were introduced to our group.

As the evening drew to a close and the members of our party began to disperse, a most attractive silver-haired gentleman with a deep tan, beautiful brown eyes, and a dazzling smile approached me. "I am Naguib MANkarious," he announced with formidable presence.

"I am Marilyn Miglin," I replied.

"I have heard about you," he said. "It is an honor to meet you."

"And I know of you," I answered. "You are married to Jewel Lafontant." I was indeed aware of his beautiful wife, a powerful international lawyer, who was celebrated by Presidents and heads of state for her professional acumen and civic contributions.

"No longer," he said, his smile diminished. "I lost her to cancer. She died last May."

"I had no idea," I apologized. "I'm terribly sorry."

"And where is your husband?" he asked.

At that moment, I felt every raw emotion surging through me. "How dare you ask me such a question!" I snapped. You know perfectly well what happened. The *world* knows what happened!"

"No. I do not know. I was with Jewel in the hospital. Taking care of her took every hour of every day. I lost track of time. I lost track of people. Only now am I becoming again social," he explained with his Egyptian accent.

Jewel and Naguib had been honored by Shaare Zedek three years previously, and he had traveled to Israel to accept the second half of the award on their behalf.

We chatted briefly, but it was late. The following day, we were to visit the Raoul Wallenberg Pediatric Day Care Hospital, where Naguib, myself, and two others were to receive a special award tribute. Exhausted and jet-lagged, I said good night and returned to my room.

The next morning proved to be fateful.

I dressed in honor of the Israeli flag—in white and powder blue. When Naguib greeted our group dressed in the same manner, I could not help but notice. Upon recognizing my own choice of attire, his eyes twinkled, and he again shared with me his beautiful smile.

"*I* will escort you," he announced.

He took my arm and from that moment on Naguib MANkarious never let go. It was a nice feeling to have a man help me off the bus and hold an umbrella over my head to protect me from the hot sun. It was nice to have a gentleman genuinely interested in my well-being.

Share Zedek is an international pediatric center that treats any child without regard to race, gender, religion, or nationality. Each member of our group brought toys for the children in the wards and we were delighted to see Arab and Israeli children playing together.

A special plaque bearing my name was ceremoniously affixed to the wall of the Plastic and Reconstructive Surgery Ward, a tribute to my work with disfigured patients. Although there were speeches and meetings with hospital administrators, it was the children who were most important to me. I made sure I spoke to each of them. It was heartbreaking to find out that many of them were wounded in wars all too common in the Middle East.

Throughout the rest of the trip, Naguib was my constant companion. He sat next to me at every dinner, beside me on each bus tour, and he gave me great reason to smile. With his dark Egyptian good-looks and charismatic charm, I felt comfortable at his side.

Everywhere we visited, our group was treated as dignitaries, courtesy of Share Zedek Hospital and the Israeli government. We were entertained by the Mayor of Jerusalem, whom Naguib knew personally. We visited Masada, where a small band of Jewish zealots held out against the Roman Army until, rather than be captured, they committed suicide.

Swimming in the Dead Sea was a comical adventure. Given the density of the salt in the water, one can only float. Later, we slathered ourselves with the sea's mud, purported to possess both medicinal and cosmetic attributes.

"I'll stick with your skin care products," Marlena concluded, as we washed off the sticky mess. That mud was one cosmetic remedy I had no intention of investigating further.

For me, the biggest cultural shock of being in that country was seeing eighteen year olds with machine guns. Israel has been at war since its founding over fifty years ago, and all citizens are required to serve in the Army upon graduating from high school.

We toured the Knesset, the Israeli Parliament. There we were escorted by former General Moshe Dyan's daughter Yael, a government official, who stayed with us for over an hour answering our questions. Afterward, I toured the Biblical Gardens—an rare honor granted by the Israeli government. There I was able to touch and smell all of the flowers mentioned in the Bible. For me, this excursion was a very special gift.

With only Rabbi Axler at my side, I visited the Avenue of the Righteous, where I planted a tree in Lee's memory. It was an important moment for me. I felt that he had indeed joined me on this journey we had planned to enjoy together, and that in this holy place—dedicated to those who had braved the evil of the world by giving of themselves—the sapling I planted for him would grow to symbolize his strength and dignity.

To my surprise, I found that it was not difficult for me to talk about Lee's death with Naguib. The great care he took in listening to every word and emotion I shared was genuine. I felt very much at ease in his company.

"I, too, know what is like to lose someone I loved," he confided. "My heart has been heavy and I felt that life had no meaning for me any longer. I have gone about my affairs, tending to my business, but things are not the same."

There was definitely an immediate rapport between us. We had each lost the one person in the world who had mattered most, our respective soul mates. Almost without words, we seemed to understand one another.

As our tour continued, Naguib, a great historian and storyteller, often acted as our guide, describing the multitude of cultures in Israel and pointing out various landmarks of interest. An international business consultant, he had garnered an impressive reputation in negotiating important business development between foreign countries. If ever there was an individual who defined the phrase "a man of the world," it was Naguib. Fluent in twelve languages, he recognized the necessity of building trust in order to foster global relations. As an international consultant, the secret to his success, he explained, was his ability to understand the mindsets on both sides of the table.

"My American clients cannot understand why they are unable to close deals over the phone," he sighed. "I have to explain to them that outside the United States, it is important that the people see you and speak with you. You must make personal assurances and be patient."

Conversely, it was Naguib's experience that the foreign bureaucrats with whom he negotiated sometimes had unrealistic expectations. "They want everything their way and are used to getting it," he said. "I am able to make them understand that in international business, give and take is necessary. If they are not willing to give a little, they will get nothing. I am able to compromise between the American ways and the local customs. I understand both sides better than each can do alone."

As we continued our tour, I particularly looked forward to visiting Petra. Before arriving in Israel, my Chicago alderman had insisted that I visit the famed Turkish baths. "Alderman Natarus," I had admonished him good naturedly, "a lady does *not* visit a Turkish bath."

When I mentioned this to Naguib on the bus, however, he proclaimed, "*I* will take you to the baths."

Unfortunately, we arrived in Petra at 9:30 p.m., and to my disappointment, the baths were closed.

Naguib would not hear of this.

With his formidable manner, he persuaded the owner of our hotel to assemble those necessary to open the baths just for me. Needless to say, I was embarrassed, and yet charmed.

"For *you*," he announced triumphantly, "the baths will be reopened."

A small group of us, including Duke and Rabbi Axler, entered the baths and with great trepidation and modesty, I carefully made my way in a pink towel to the steam room. There, Naguib insisted upon rubbing my weary feet, maintaining, "*All* beautiful women *must* have their feet rubbed." Then, in Arabic, he ordered me into the next room for a massage.

Straining my eyes through the steam to make my way into a massage room, I passed the Rabbi, who was enjoying a shower. He noticed my presence at precisely the same moment I realized the circumstances.

"Oh my," I apologized, turning crimson. "I'll just turn my back."

If I had not been sufficiently mortified at this embarrassing encounter, I was further humbled upon the making the acquaintance of my masseur, who appeared to have been all of twelve or thirteen years old. With one deft sweep of the hand, he pulled away my towel and began a vigorous massage I shall never forget.

Afterwards, dressed in white robes with towels wrapped around our heads—Turkish style—we regrouped in the parlor to compare our experiences.

The following evening, Naguib and I slipped away from the group for cocktails in the hotel. I found myself very comfortable with him, and only then did I begin to realize just how lonely I had become. In his presence, there seemed to be more light than I had seen in over a year.

When finally we ended our trip in Tel Aviv, Naguib seized a microphone at a restaurant and made a startling declaration. In his charming Egyptian accent, he announced: "I 'felt' in love with this beautiful woman—Maraleen Miglin. I must ask her to marry me."

The entire group was stunned into silence. So was I.

Every head swiveled toward me, awaiting a reaction. "Oh, my!" was all I managed to utter, while struggling to maintain my composure. Experiencing such a rush of emotions, I was unsure exactly how I should feel.

Upon returning to Chicago, we continued to see one another and I found myself looking forward to the time we spent together. He held my hand on walks and escorted me to dinner. He was outgoing and romantic, taking great pleasure in sharing his feelings with all who would listen.

The Chicago press was indeed listening. Our courtship quickly became fodder for the gossip columnists who breathlessly reported upon the commonality of our respective tragedies. "Could Marilyn Miglin be headed for the altar?" they asked.

"No, no," I told friends and family, downplaying my growing relationship with Naguib. "I am not getting married, but it is nice to have such a handsome gentleman as an escort," I admitted.

Naguib was not one to give up easily.

Everything he did, was executed with exuberance, and grandeur. Ultimately, he had decided that we were meant to be together forever. "Maraleen, we must marry soon. We cannot wait. I 'felt' in love with you." That phrase, spoken with his Egyptian accent emphasizing the word "felt" rather than "fell" would continue to charm me whenever he boomed his declaration of love.

He was slowly wearing me down.

My decision to remarry was one of the most difficult I have ever made in my life. For months, I struggled to sort my feelings, enduring incredible angst. But increasingly, I recognized the strength that I derived from Naguib's company.

One evening, over dinner at the Ritz Carlton, he hid an engagement ring in my dessert and again publicly declared his love. I could no longer resist the companionship he was offering me, and when I accepted the ring, the entire dining room burst into applause.

The next day, the details of my special evening were shared with the entire city of Chicago, courtesy of a gossip columnist. Naguib was delighted with the story. I, on the other hand, had carefully avoided the press since Lee's death. The renewed attention regarding my personal life was something I did not particularly relish. I was not certain of how the general public would accept the news of my engagement only fifteen months later.

Naguib was incorrigible, however, in his desire to make his feelings for me known.

In March of 1999, the Illinois Eye Bank bestowed upon me their "Woman of Vision" award at an elegant dinner ceremony.

With Naguib at the Woman of Vision dinner

With my dashing Egyptian prince at my side, impeccably dressed in his tuxedo, we enjoyed greeting many friends and associates I had not seen in over a year. Their genuine enthusiasm for my renewed happiness was deeply touching.

After being presented with my award by Illinois Secretary of State Jessie White, who shared a tribute from the Governor, we danced and visited with each of our guests. Making our way from table to table, I introduced Naguib to everyone. Between their congratulations and compliments, the one question of the evening was, "When are you getting married?"

Before I could respond, Naguib proudly answered, "She will marry me very soon."

Shortly thereafter, I felt it was necessary to formally introduce my fiancé to my Oak Street staff. For months, they had witnessed Naguib escorting me to and from the Institute. His endless pronouncement of, "I *love* this beautiful woman" was difficult to avoid overhearing upon each of his entrances, but they knew little about him. A simple introduction, however, was not Naguib's style.

He arranged for a sumptuous dinner celebration at the Drake Hotel's International Club. True to his nature, he attended to every last detail to orchestrate an unforgettable evening for everyone.

In a private dining room, I introduced Naguib to my staff. When at last the introductions were finished, he waved his hand and announced, "It is with pleasure I make formally the acquaintance of each of you. You are like a member of a close family to her," he continued, "and your presence in her life is of great importance to me."

He motioned to the head waiter.

"I request that you will close the doors of this room, for now I will tell to you the story of how I 'felt' in love with this beautiful woman." As if on cue, the double doors of the room swung shut and my staff fell silent, waiting for him to continue.

"My wife and I," he said, "had been honored by Shaare Zedek in Jerusalem with the Raoul Wallenberg Award. Several years later, when Marilyn Miglin was honored with this very award, I was invited on a trip to Israel with previous award honorees.

"Although my heart was empty, I considered that by taking this journey to Jerusalem, I would honor my wife's memory. I thought it would be good to escape this sadness of my life in Chicago.

"I agreed to travel with this group of people and act as their surrogate guide to a world new to most of them. What I did not know was anything about her," he said, gesturing to me at the opposite end of the table.

Never had I heard him speak of our introduction with such eloquence.

283

"She was a message from God, full of life and energy. In this instant, I knew that I would find happiness in being with her.

"When she explained to me the circumstances of her husband's death, I then knew that we were meant to be together. I told her that I, too, knew of what it was to live with a broken heart."

There was silence at the table. Satisfied with his dramatic telling of our first meeting, Naguib, ever the eloquent story-teller, seized the moment.

"For months I have asked for her to please make me the happiest man in the world again by being my wife so that I may devote my life to her. Until now she has resisted my requests."

Naguib looked about the room, savoring the moment.

"I request that with your good assistance, she will agree this evening to set a date for a beautiful wedding."

Every eye in the room turned to me.

I borrowed from the drama he had created, pausing for effect.

"Well, Mr. MANkarious," I answered, "we shall continue to *discuss* it."

My staff applauded.

His face lit up like that of a child on Christmas morning. "Did I tell you that I love you?" he declared.

I wanted a quiet wedding without having the press reminding me of the previous year's pain. The news of our marriage was a hot topic, and I was determined not to let the media interrupt our special day.

On May 30, 1999, I closed my Oak Street store for the first time in thirty-six years, temporarily moving the daily operations across the street. I had decided to totally remodel the salon, putting the past behind me. It was time to embrace the energy of the new millennium and take the Institute with me into the future. It was time to move forward with my life and business.

While the salon was being renovated, I did my best to manage my Egyptian "handful." I should have realized by this time, however, that nothing my incorrigible fiancé did was subtle.

He sent invitations to the press.

While I had done my best to keep the ceremony small and private, Naguib was arranging media coverage for the fanfare he felt I deserved. One week before the wedding, I was shocked to find my photo on the front page of a Chicago newspaper, along with a story that provided the intimate details of our wedding plans for the entire city to read. There it was in print—the date, time, and location.

At first I was concerned that the press would again dredge up the specter of Lee's death when writing about his widow's plans for a new marriage.

"Why do you want to keep this from the newspapers? I want to shout it out to the world!" Naguib boasted. Scissors in hand, he carefully cut out each mention of our nuptials, pasting them into a scrapbook in which he was preparing to record our forthcoming life together.

"I want the world to know that I love you," he insisted. "Let everyone know that you and I have discovered a happiness we thought impossible. I will shout it to everyone who will listen and it will come from my heart."

We chose the date of June 11, Naguib's birthday, to be married. For months, he meticulously planned our honeymoon in Egypt and grew more excited each day.

"I will introduce you to my family and friends. In Egypt, you will be treated like a queen."

In my newly remodeled store with Bobbie Rae Carter (center) and a member of my staff.

With my perfumer, Vito Lenoci

Three generations—Marlena, me, and Helen

As our excitement grew, so did the guest list. What was originally planned as an intimate affair for our immediate families
was now escalating into a large event.

It didn't matter. I was happy.

The emotion of renewed hope is indeed intoxicating. Without this, life becomes a meaningless exercise. For the first time
since Lee's death and the ordeal that followed, I felt a surge of
anticipation. I was now looking forward to the future.

The morning of the wedding, I looked out from the kitchen
windows to the elegant tables draped with ivory linens in my
garden. Each table was topped with a magnificent arrangement
of peonies in anticipation of over one-hundred-fifty guests.

287

The wedding cake was exquisite. Marlena had chosen it for us with all the love in her heart.

Helen, Marion, and Virge arrived, requesting that I personally apply their makeup. They looked beautiful and my heart swelled with pride. The men in the wedding party struggled to pin on their boutonnieres as I helped secure corsages on my mother, aunts, and the others who were part of the ceremony.

"Today I am the luckiest man in the world," I heard Naguib call from the driveway. "This is the happiest day of my life. I am marrying the most beautiful woman anyone has seen."

By this time, nearly everyone had left for the church. Heart pounding, I finally stepped out to greet him. He looked at me with such love and pride in his eyes.

"I love you," he said, taking my hand and kissing it. "You are like an angel."

Arm and arm we floated outside, through the garden, and to the chauffeured car. When he opened the door, I could not believe what I was seeing. Lining the floor and the inside of the town car were literally thousands upon thousands of rose petals.

"You are perfect, like a rose," he whispered, "and only such perfection will now touch my wife."

I was now sure that I was in a fairy tale, just as I had imagined when I was a child.

We were married in the same glorious Polish cathedral with soaring Gothic arches that my grandmother had taken me to as a child. Unseasonable temperatures in the mid-nineties began heating up the church that morning. Unfortunately, there was no air-conditioning and our guests began fanning themselves briskly and dabbing at the perspiration on their faces. Not Naguib. He remained cool, impeccably tailored, his handshake steady as the pyramids.

Father Robert McLaughlin of Holy Name Cathedral officiated. Naguib, a Coptic Christian, also arranged for his good
friend Reverend John Buchanan from Fourth Presbyterian
Church to share in the blessing.

When my ninety-eight year old mother-in-law Anna Miglin
was carried up the stairs of the church in her wheelchair, I truly
felt honored and blessed. She had ridden in a car for hours to
attend. Her beautiful blue eyes sparkled like Lee's and her presence on that day made me feel as though Lee's energy was there
as well, protecting and encouraging me to embrace this found
joy.

The actual ceremony was short, but magical. And so, again,
I was married.

Aside from the unexpected heat, it was a perfect day. After
the last of the guests departed from our garden reception, a tor-
rential downpour cooled down the weather. Naguib and I
gathered together our luggage for our Egyptian honeymoon.

The limousine driver beamed as we again sat among the still
fragrant rose petals. Through a thunderstorm, and bumper to
bumper traffic, we advanced toward the airport and our new
life together.

Whether or not the crew aboard our United Airlines flight
knew who we were, I do not know. Yet, I learned whenever I was
with Naguib never to be surprised by the wonderful response
accorded our presence.

We had been upgraded to first class, and the pilot himself
presented us with a bottle of champagne and a huge vase of flowers from United Airlines. It was a lovely gesture, but the
arrangement was so enormous the crew was forced to store it in
the cockpit.

"For you," my new husband reminded me, "only the best."

The next morning we landed in Frankfort two hours behind schedule, too late to connect with our flight to Alexandria. As a lovely agent whisked us through the busy terminal for a connecting flight to Cairo, I pleaded, "Please, please do not lose our luggage!"

Not to worry, we were assured. It would indeed be transferred to our new destination.

Upon our arrival in Cairo, however, our luggage was nowhere to be found. To my dismay, we were told that there were only three flights to Alexandria each week. The prospect of seeing my baggage and the beautiful clothes I had packed for my honeymoon anytime in the near future seemed unlikely.

It reminded me of the trip Lee and I had taken to Rome. I could only hope that I would be blessed with similar ensuing adventure. I was not to be disappointed.

We arrived in Alexandria at two a.m. the following morning. The hotel and suite, which Naguib had arranged was more luxurious and grand than I could ever have imagined. Each room was filled with roses and the arrangement of food that greeted us was a veritable buffet—more than any two people could possibly eat. Knowing of my guilty pleasure of enjoying potato chips, he had also arranged for ten different brands to be included on the table.

Naguib escorted me to the balcony overlooking the Mediterranean Sea—I was amazed. It was the size of my entire house! When at last we retired, completely exhausted from our journey, I heard the distinctive buzz of a mosquito inside the canopied bed.

"I will take care of it," huffed Naguib, clearly as irritated as I.

"No! No!" I protested. "Don't kill it!"

He turned to look at me in amazement.

I cannot stand to see the soul of anything destroyed, including insects. Although it may seem extreme to others, I have developed a skill for catching errant flies under a glass and then release them outdoors.

Naguib was incredulous. "You wish for me to catch this mosquito and set it free?"

I nodded. He sighed in resignation and proceeded to wander about the suite, chasing after our unexpected visitor. When finally our flying friend was freed from the room, we settled ourselves and dozed off to sleep.

The following morning, we awakened to the sun shining brightly upon the shimmering Mediterranean. Over breakfast on the balcony, Naguib shared with me the details of the itinerary he had spent so many hours preparing. I could not help but be charmed by his childlike exuberance in introducing me to his friends and family.

We were reunited with our luggage in Cairo the following day. The city was just as I had remembered—hot, bustling, noisy and oh, so beautiful and traditional. He had arranged for another wondrous suite at the Oberoi Hotel, the former palace of King Farouk. We were greeted by an acquaintance of Naguib's named Lily, a lovely woman, who showed us to our stunning apartment of rooms overlooking the pyramids. The ceilings were forty-feet high and the magnificent bed was both formidable and regal. As usual, Naguib had arranged for baskets of flowers, fresh fruits, and a stunning assortment of delicious food.

He was a seasoned world traveler, and life with him was like a fairy tale where I was the princess and he the prince. With his fluent Arabic, immaculate dress and mannerisms, Naguib commanded attention from royalty and servants alike. In Egypt, he was always referred to by the respectful title of "Pasha."

After a camel ride with private guides to the pyramids, we drove to one of the poorest villages near Cairo to find the smallest church I have ever seen. We wound our way up steep, narrow steps to a small altar where three orthodox priests and two altar boys were waiting for us. There was music in the background being played on ancient instruments as Naguib's boyhood priest, Father Agantha, blessed us.

We then departed for a grand celebration aboard a yacht on the Nile. Sailing along the river, I turned to Naguib. "This is all so beautiful. Everything you planned has been wonderful. How did you know how to make me so happy?" I asked.

"Everything must always be perfect for my wife," he replied, smiling.

That memorable evening we hosted a dinner party in our suite for his immediate family—twenty smiling, delightful people. The women begged me to allow them to examine my nightgowns and jewelry, and before they left, I taught each of them how to properly apply their makeup.

By the time our guests had departed, I was exhausted. The patio doors had been left open, and we finally slipped into bed to the sound of a family of mosquitos. I hoped they would take pity upon us this time, and allowed their high-pitched buzzing to lull me to sleep.

The next morning I was weary and irritable.

"Now, Marilyn," said my perpetually tanned husband, "you must come to rest with me on the beach."

I am certainly not a beach girl, but everything else he had planned had been so marvelous. How could I say no?

He took me to a private cabana near the water, actually a small, elegant apartment. When I looked around, however, I saw five pairs of eyes staring at me.

"Naguib! Who are these men? Please ask them to leave." My mood was rapidly changing, since I did not want to share my cabin with five strangers.

On our honeymoon in Egypt

"No, no, Marilyn, these men are all here to serve you, all of them," Naguib reassured me. "They need this job. This is how they support their families."

So one swept the some specks of sand from the white marble floors, which were already spotlessly clean. Another of the men poured water for us to drink, another fixed my chair, and another cleaned the toilet each time it was used. The fifth man took our order for lunch.

This luxury brought me back to reality, as I realized these men needed their jobs to survive. During our trip, the blessings of my own life were constantly reinforced.

By then, all I wanted to do was settle down and read a book. Despite five umbrellas that Naguib had positioned around me as protection from the Egyptian sun, I developed a second-degree burn over my entire face.

That evening we went to a glorious high-society garden party, one of the most sophisticated I have ever attended. It took place behind a high wall, with musicians playing classical music, and unbelievable mounds of food, superbly prepared and served. The guests, were elegantly attired. The women glittered in spectacular jewelry, and there I was with a very sunburned face.

Every day Naguib had planned to perfection—early morning breakfasts overlooking the Nile, a private faluka boat ride on the river, a picnic on a private island. He had my hands and feet hennaed, and arranged for the fulfillment of my every whim.

Before we returned to Chicago, I would visit twenty-seven families, each of them in different locations, each of them offering a feast of Egyptian specialties. Every evening included dinner, dancing under the stars, and carriage rides.

Our life could not have been more perfect.

At home, Naguib remained as irrepressible and romantic as ever. He insisted upon traveling everywhere with me, often accompanying me to the Home Shopping Network. During one of my appearances there, while speaking on camera about the ingredients of Pheromone, I turned to find my husband had joined me on air.

"Ladies," he said, "It was Marilyn's perfume that made me 'felt' in love with this beautiful woman. It is a wonderful fragrance and you *must* buy it."

Then, before an audience of millions, he pulled me to him and kissed me!

I don't know how the Network producer and executives felt about this, but the ladies loved it. My Pheromone configurations sold out in a matter of moments.

In the early 1990s, Lee and I had served as the Illinois delegates to the Board of Directors for the Kennedy Center for the Performing Arts in Washington, D.C. We enjoyed working with this impressive group of people, many of whom became good friends.

After his death, my involvement with the Kennedy Center was only one of a series of commitments which I found impossible to continue. It was with sadness, but necessity, that I let my membership in this important organization drop.

During the next year, I lost touch with many of the members, although I often thought of the group we had worked with. Shortly after my marriage to Naguib, I was delighted to receive a message from the Kennedy Center, congratulating me on my new happiness. Furthermore, this dynamic board knew of Naguib's connections in international circles as well as in Washington, D.C., and invited him to become a member.

It was with great pride that this Egyptian-born man accepted a role in shaping our nation's performing arts, and as his wife, I was honored again to serve on the Board of Directors.

Together, Naguib and I planned an elegant soirée welcoming the committee members to our home. As usual, he insisted on attending to every last detail, ensuring a perfect evening. He charmed our guests with fascinating tales of international travels, foreign diplomacy, and global protocol.

Never had they encountered such a roguishly charming character. That evening, I found tremendous satisfaction in knowing, that together, Naguib and I were only beginning our new life together.

As winter settled over the city, Naguib elected to have some minor surgery. He wished to have some sagging skin removed from under his eyes and an Egyptian doctor friend had been telling him for years that he could make him look ten years younger. The doctor finally convinced him to have a little nip and tuck.

"Don't worry," he reassured me. "You do not need to be with me for such a little thing. I do not want for you to see me with bandages."

His doctor scheduled the surgery on his day off. As I was committed to giving a previously scheduled speech to the Young Executives Club, there was nothing I could do other than encourage him to relax and follow his doctor's instructions.

That evening, Marlena, Duke and I had a dinner discussion regarding a new business opportunity we had been working on for quite some time. We enjoyed a marvelous dinner on Michigan Avenue, reassuring each other that it was a time for only good things to happen as the new century unfolded.

We can hope for the best, but we never know what fate holds for each of us at any time. Our lives are constantly changing— we may never understand why, but we must live with the outcome.

After saying good night to my friends and children, I returned home to find the answering machine blinking rapidly. Removing my coat, I pressed the "play" button, grabbing a pen from the kitchen counter to transcribe the recordings. I was not prepared for the series of messages that followed.

The first call was from Naguib's physician. His voice was full of concern. "Please call me as soon as possible," he said.

Another message followed, the doctor's voice sounding more desperate, "It's important that you call me as soon as you get home."

This was followed by another message from the hospital, which I turned off before listening to all of it.

As I called Marlena and then Duke, my hands were beginning to shake.

"Something has happened," I managed to say, a feeling of dread entering my heart.

I was overcome with a familiar feeling of foreboding. The room seemed to be moving around me. Then, before I could return the doctor's call, the phone rang. I grabbed for the receiver, hoping that it was Naguib calling to tell me that everything was all right.

The voice on the other end of the phone quietly told me that Naguib was dead. He had died from unforeseen complications following the surgery.

I was dumbfounded. How could this be happening yet again?

Only that morning, my handsome Egyptian prince had repeated the words he had told me over and over again during our brief marriage, "Did I tell you that I love you?"

Fifteen hours earlier in the brightness of the morning light, he had kissed me and laughing, said, "When next you see me, I shall be as beautiful as you."

How could he be gone?

What happened to my wondrous fairy tale? Our life together was just beginning. I had only rediscovered happiness and passion. I was now walking backwards, again reliving the most painful journey in my life for a *second* time.

How could I trudge along that path of heartache yet again?

It was not a matter of being strong and stoic in the face of renewed tragedy. All I could do was my best to get through each hour. There were phone calls and arrangements to be made. With the assistance of Duke and Marlena, I numbly began doing what needed to be done, but I was functioning on autopilot.

The hours passed, and then it was morning. I hadn't slept at all.

As usual, there were the newspapers and television cameras to contend with. Our attempts to maintain order, dignity, and calm were instead met with the headline: "Murder Spree Widow Faces Second Tragedy."

There it was, reminding me of every painful moment I had struggled to overcome and put behind me. My life had come full circle, and there was nothing I could do but continue to hold my head above the gossip and insistent nosiness of those who wished only to further capitalize upon my heartbreak.

At first I was determined to have a private service to shield Naguib's sons and my own family from the renewed glare of the spotlight. Further reflection, however, brought to mind a flood of memories of my brief time together with Naguib, a man beloved, admired, and respected by many. It was only fitting to honor him with a service celebrating his accomplishments and love of life.

As I learned from Lee's death, people need an outlet to express their grief and sorrow. As painful as a public service would be, I knew that it was necessary for our friends and family to find some semblance of closure befitting this man who lived with such grand style.

Hundreds gathered at the Fourth Presbyterian Church. Heads of state, civic and business leaders, and friends eulogized this man whose spirit was so all-encompassing. It was as though Naguib himself were looking down from high above the soaring ceiling of the cathedral, approvingly nodding, "Yes, this is good."

And then it was over. As quickly as our whirlwind romance had begun, it had abruptly ended.

Was I to retreat into seclusion to console my broken heart? The endless inquiries from reporters constantly reminded me of the public's curiosity for what I would do next.

"Can you tell me if Ms. Miglin will be traveling abroad now?" My office was inundated by such calls. "We heard she will be leaving for Europe for several months."

I could hide in Europe if I wanted to. No one would blame me for the need to escape such glaring, unwanted attention. But, I have never run from anything. I have never allowed difficulties to determine the manner in which I choose to embrace the life God has given me.

I had been through too much to give up now.

The business I had devoted myself to for so many years needed my guidance, my family and friends needed me for love and support, and the many projects I was involved with needed completion. I was scheduled for television appearances, and if I canceled them, this would only bring problems for the Home Shopping Network, and frustration to my customers.

I needed to immediately begin the process of healing my heart and soul in the only way I knew how—by putting my best face forward in the most positive manner I could.

Both Lee and Naguib embraced and celebrated life. That is what I knew I had to do, not only for myself, but to honor their memories.

As painful as each day could be, I stayed busy, throwing my energy into various projects that would help others. This was the lesson I had originally learned when Lee died, and this is how I still cope today.

I take life ten minutes at a time, then an hour at a time, and then finally, a day at a time.

Only God knows the future of every one of us, and we must enjoy and live every moment to its fullest because life can be all too brief. I never question what the universe holds. I believe that God works in wondrous ways.

Rose Kennedy once said, "After a storm, the birds still sing."

Meeting the Dali Lama, a great spiritual leader

Aboard an aircraft carrier with members of the Board for the Performing Arts

The birds sing, the sun still rises, and life is filled with joy when we take the opportunity to look for it. Like a prisoner in a cell, it is easy to become accustomed to the dark, and fearful of the sun's blinding brightness.

I, however, still believe in fairy tales. I believe in angels and in looking forward to the rewards that life brings.

Find the splendor within your soul by continuing to dream. Test the strength of your will by striving to live each day in the most positive manner you can. Find the courage for victories through the magic of believing.

"The past is a place you can visit—but you cannot stay."